Resilient Students

Build resilience in your students, starting in the elementary grades, so they develop the skills to overcome challenges and thrive in school and beyond.

Bestselling author Dr. Brad Johnson presents a strength-based approach to resilience, showing that it's much more than bouncing back but involves adapting and growing along the way. He shows the best ways to foster resilience in kids by teaching them grit, emotional intelligence, a growth mindset, and the ability to embrace failure, all while uncovering and building their strengths and confidence. He also reveals why this is such a key skill for our changing world.

Written in Brad's signature accessible style, the book offers loads of practical takeaways so you can get started building a more resilient classroom today!

Brad Johnson is one of the most dynamic and engaging speakers in the fields of education and leadership. He has over 30 years of experience in the trenches as a teacher and administrator. He is the author of many books including *Dear Teacher*, *Principal Bootcamp*, *Putting Teachers First,* and *Becoming a More Assertive Teacher*. He has travelled the globe speaking and training teachers and educational leaders.

Also Available from Brad Johnson & Routledge Eye On Education
www.routledge.com/k-12

Becoming a More Assertive Teacher: Maximizing Strengths, Establishing Boundaries, and Amplifying Your Voice

Finding Your Leadership Edge: Balancing Assertiveness and Compassion in Schools

Dear Teacher: 100 Days of Inspirational Quotes and Anecdotes
with Hal Bowman

Thank You, Teacher: 100 Uplifting and Affirming Letters from Your Fellow Educators
with Hal Bowman

Finding Your Leadership Edge: Balancing Assertiveness and Compassion in Schools

Principal Bootcamp:
Accelerated Strategies to Influence and Lead from Day One

Putting Teachers First:
How to Inspire, Motivate, and Connect with Your Staff

Learning On Your Feet, 2e:
Incorporating Physical Activity into the K-8 Classroom
with Melody Jones

What Schools Don't Teach:
20 Ways to Help Students Excel in School and in Life
with Julie Sessions

From School Administrator to School Leader:
15 Keys to Maximizing Your Leadership Potential
with Julie Sessions

Dear School Leader: 50 Motivational Quotes and Anecdotes that Affirm Your Purpose and Your Impact

Resilient Students

Building Life Skills in the K-5 Classroom and Beyond

Brad Johnson

Routledge
Taylor & Francis Group
NEW YORK AND LONDON

Designed cover image: Getty Images

First published 2026
by Routledge
605 Third Avenue, New York, NY 10158

and by Routledge
4 Park Square, Milton Park, Abingdon, Oxon, OX14 4RN

Routledge is an imprint of the Taylor & Francis Group, an informa business

© 2026 Brad Johnson

The right of Brad Johnson to be identified as author of this work has been asserted in accordance with sections 77 and 78 of the Copyright, Designs and Patents Act 1988.

All rights reserved. No part of this book may be reprinted or reproduced or utilised in any form or by any electronic, mechanical, or other means, now known or hereafter invented, including photocopying and recording, or in any information storage or retrieval system, without permission in writing from the publishers.

Trademark notice: Product or corporate names may be trademarks or registered trademarks, and are used only for identification and explanation without intent to infringe.

ISBN: 978-1-041-07392-5 (hbk)
ISBN: 978-1-041-07391-8 (pbk)
ISBN: 978-1-003-64026-4 (ebk)

DOI: 10.4324/9781003640264

Typeset in Palatino
by Newgen Publishing UK

Dedication
Thank you, teachers!

Contents

Meet the Author viii

Introduction: The Power of Resilience 1

1 Resilience—A Life Skill Built on the Playground and Beyond 3

2 Rewiring Our Brains to Handle Challenges 13

3 Teaching "Not Yet" and Growth Mindset 23

4 Tapping into Students' Unique Strengths 33

5 Fostering Emotional Awareness and Intelligence 41

6 Encouraging Students to Learn from Failure 51

7 Building Autonomy and Self-Regulation 59

8 Harnessing the Power of Play and Physical Activity 71

9 Creating a Classroom Culture of Resilience 84

10 Resilience: A Blueprint for Adapting to a Changing World 96

References 106

Meet the Author

Dr. Brad Johnson is a globally recognised educational leader, speaker, and author with over 30 years of experience in transforming schools. Ranked #3 among the top 30 Global Gurus in Education, Dr. Johnson is passionate about empowering educators to maximise their potential through strong relationships, communication, and collaboration. Author of 15 influential books, including *Finding Your Leadership Edge*, *Becoming a More Assertive Teacher*, and the bestseller *Dear Teacher*, Dr. Johnson offers practical guidance for educators at all levels. His work is rooted in relational intelligence and servant leadership, helping school leaders build authentic, trust-based connections with their teams. A highly sought-after speaker, Dr. Johnson has presented in 12 countries and is the host of the *Lattes with Leaders* podcast. He inspires educators worldwide with his message of leadership that not only builds resilient teams but also brings out the brilliance in every child. His work demonstrates the transformative power of leadership that prioritises people, creating lasting positive change in schools and communities. For speaking availability or more information about Dr. Johnson's work, visit www.DoctorBradJohnson.com

Introduction: The Power of Resilience

It's the middle of a writing lesson, and Lily's pencil is frozen in midair. She stares at the blank page in front of her, her eyes welling up with frustration. "I don't know what to write," she whispers. A few minutes later, her classmate Noah is facing the same challenge—he can't think of how to start either. But instead of trying again, Noah crumples the paper and slumps in his chair. "I just can't do this," he mutters, pushing his paper aside.

Across the room, Lily's still sitting, but instead of giving up, she taps her pencil, rereads the prompt, and scribbles a few words. "This might not be perfect," she says softly, "but I'll fix it later." She doesn't let frustration stop her; she keeps going.

What makes the difference? Resilience.

Resilience is more than just pushing through challenges—it's the ability to adapt, recover, and keep going, even when things feel difficult. It's what helps students like Lily take risks, learn from mistakes, and develop confidence in their ability to grow.

And the good news? Resilience isn't something kids either have or don't have—it's something we can teach.

And it's one of the most important lessons we can teach.

Resilience has always been a critical skill for success. Throughout history, individuals have had to persevere through adversity to achieve their goals, whether it was overcoming personal challenges or tackling societal obstacles. But as we look to the future, resilience is more important than ever. The world is evolving at an unprecedented pace—technological advances, shifting job markets, global challenges, and social changes are all part of the landscape students will inherit. The ability to adapt, bounce back from setbacks, and keep moving forward will be essential for success in a world that is constantly changing.

The students sitting in your classroom today will grow up to face challenges far beyond school—job interviews that don't go their way, setbacks in relationships, and unexpected hardships. Life will throw obstacles at them, just as it does to all of us. The question isn't whether they'll face difficulties, but whether they'll have the skills to push through them.

That's why what we do now matters.

When we teach our students to keep going when they're frustrated, to see mistakes as part of learning, and to believe in their own ability to grow, we're giving them more than just academic skills—we're giving them life skills. We're shaping the kind of adults they will become. Adults who won't crumble under pressure, who won't see failure as the end, but as a stepping stone to something greater.

This book is your practical guide to fostering resilience in K-5 students—through growth mindset, emotional intelligence, perseverance, and play. You'll find strategies that fit seamlessly into your daily routine and stories that remind you why your role as an educator is so powerful.

So, take a deep breath, grab your coffee, and let's dive in. Together, we'll create a classroom where resilience isn't just taught—it's lived.

1
Resilience—A Life Skill Built on the Playground and Beyond

Remember those wild, carefree days on the playground? Long before tests and homework took center stage, we learned our most important life lessons amid scraped knees, dizzy spins on the merry-go-round, and the thrill of climbing that daunting 12-foot slide. It was on those dusty patches of ground, with no formal lessons on perseverance—only our own grit and determination—that we discovered the truth: falling down isn't a failure; it's a chance to rise again, stronger than before.

Research by Dr. Peter Gray (2013), a psychologist and expert on child development, shows that children who engage in unstructured play on the playground develop better problem-solving skills and more emotional resilience. His research shows that children need these experiences to learn persistence and self-regulation, which are crucial for facing life's challenges later on. Without them, kids may struggle to bounce back when they encounter obstacles in the future.

The Playground: Our First School of Resilience

Learning Through Play
Think back to the days when a tumble on the playground was just another adventure. There were no cushioned corners or official pep talks—only laughter, a few bruises, and that unspoken promise to get back up. Whether it was missing a jump rope beat or losing a race, each fall taught us that trying again was part of the fun. These experiences laid the groundwork for a resilience that lasts a lifetime.

The essence of resilience is not simply getting back up after a fall—it is learning to take risks, understanding that failure is part of growth, and developing the perseverance to keep moving forward. On the playground, kids practice risk-taking constantly, whether it's testing their own limits in a race, challenging themselves on a jungle gym, or pushing the boundaries of their social circles. This early exposure to failure and the opportunity to try again is the foundation of emotional resilience.

The Merry-Go-Round of Grit
If the playground were a classroom for life, the merry-go-round was its most daring teacher. Not the gentle spin you'd expect—but the wild, heart-pounding ride that had you gripping the cold metal for dear life. Remember those moments when the ride suddenly sped up, and you were flung off, scraping your knee or even ripping a hole in the knee of your favorite jeans? Those mishaps were more than just accidents—they were proof that, sometimes, you have to get a little messy before you can learn how to hold on tight. Every time we got thrown off, we learned that it wasn't about avoiding the ride but about mustering the courage to dust ourselves off, nurse our scraped knees, and jump right back on for another go.

As educators, we can help students develop their own "merry-go-round moments" by providing opportunities for risk-taking and problem-solving, allowing them to experience setbacks and then bounce back from them. This is essential for cultivating grit, the perseverance to persist even when faced with obstacles.

The 12-foot Slide: The Lesson of Bravery
Then there was the towering 12-foot slide. Its metal surface gleamed under the harsh sun, daring us to climb its high ladder. As we reached the top, there was always that moment—a mix of dread and thrill—when we sat down, legs pressed against the scalding metal. Sliding down was inevitable, but the landing? That was the unknown.

If you didn't fall and break your ankle on the climb up, you were in for a whole different kind of pain. Sliding down that hot metal? It wasn't just the height that scared you—it was the third-degree burns waiting to happen. The sting of the metal against your legs was like a fire drill for your skin. But despite all that, the temptation was too strong. You'd climb back up for another ride.

With each fall, we learned something important: resilience isn't about avoiding rough landings or burns; it's about accepting them—and then laughing about it! After all, even if you ended up with a charred backside, you still stood tall, brushed yourself off, and said, "I'll do it again." Because that's what bravery is all about—taking risks, feeling the sting, and coming back for more!

Red Rover: The Power of Persistence
Who could forget the excitement (and occasional tumble) during a game of Red Rover? With hearts pounding and legs sprinting, we learned that whether you broke through or got bumped back, the true win was in daring to try. It wasn't about the outcome but the determination to keep moving forward.

Persistence is not always about immediate success; it's about sustaining the effort, even when things don't go as planned. In a classroom, this can be mirrored in tasks where the emphasis is placed on the effort put forth rather than the result. Encouraging students to give their best effort, even when the outcome is uncertain, reinforces the importance of perseverance.

The Swings: Trust, Letting Go, and Soaring High
Swings taught us something magical about trust. As we soared higher, there came that exhilarating moment when you had to

let go and trust the swing (and gravity!) to carry you safely back. It was a lesson in taking risks and embracing the unknown, knowing that a safe landing awaited.

In the classroom, building trust with students is essential for them to feel confident enough to take risks. When students trust that their efforts will be met with understanding and encouragement, they are more likely to embrace challenges head-on and persevere through adversity.

Exploring the Depths of Resilience

We learned resilience on the playground without even knowing it—racing down slides, enduring scraped knees, and laughing off tumbles. Those wild, carefree moments were our first lessons in bouncing back, even if we didn't have a fancy term for it. But times have changed. While our biggest worry was finishing a game of kickball, today's young students face pressures like early academic assessments and standardized testing even in kindergarten.

So, what exactly is resilience? Simply put, **resilience is the ability to recover from setbacks, adapt to change, and keep moving forward with confidence**. It's the inner strength that transforms failures into valuable lessons, turning challenges into opportunities for growth.

Resilience goes far beyond just bouncing back from a fall. It's the emotional strength that lets us shrug off disappointments, the mental flexibility that helps us adjust when things don't go as planned, and the willingness to learn from every twist and turn. Think of it as an inner engine that converts setbacks into stepping stones—a chance to trust our own abilities and see that failure isn't the end, but a part of the journey.

For young learners, resilience is absolutely essential. They aren't just dealing with scraped knees—they're also grappling with academic stress, social challenges, and high expectations from an early age. With structured schedules and early assessments replacing free play, these pressures can feel overwhelming. Learning resilience helps them manage stress, bounce back from disappointments, and build the confidence to explore new challenges.

And here's an important point backed by research: it's perfectly normal to experience setbacks. Studies, including those by Michi, Nolen-Hoeksema, and others, show that while failures are a natural part of life, it's when we get stuck ruminating—overthinking our mistakes—that they begin to affect our mental well-being (Michl et al., 2013). In other words, occasional failure is healthy; it's our tendency to dwell on these setbacks that can trap us in a cycle of negative thinking.

Each experience—joyful or painful—adds to a cumulative strength that shapes who we become. By understanding resilience in both its emotional and practical dimensions, we empower our students to see that every challenge contributes to a more adaptable, capable self.

Armed with this richer understanding of what resilience is, why it's so important, and how setbacks can serve as opportunities when we learn to let go of excessive rumination, let's look at how we can bring practical strategies and creative activities into our classrooms to nurture this essential life skill.

Building Resilience: Student Activities and Teacher Strategies

Developing resilience is a two-fold process—students benefit from engaging in creative, reflective activities, and teachers play a key role by modeling and reinforcing resilient behaviors. The following sections offer distinct yet complementary approaches to help students build resilience.

1. Student Creative and Reflective Activities
Building resilience in students can be done through both physical and creative challenges, allowing them to develop important

coping skills. These activities blend creativity with reflection, helping students internalize resilience in a meaningful way:

1. **Resilience Ladder:** Have students identify a personal goal and break it down into smaller, manageable steps, just like climbing a ladder. Tie this to creative tasks—such as designing a goal map or journaling—to help them visualize their progress and challenges.
2. **Mistake Art:** Encourage students to intentionally make mistakes in their artwork. This exercise teaches them that mistakes are opportunities for creativity and growth, reinforcing the idea that resilience comes from learning and adapting.
3. **Resilience Storybook:** Invite students to create their own "Resilience Storybook," illustrating moments when they overcame challenges—whether a small failure or a bigger obstacle. Sharing these stories in a class gallery walk builds empathy and helps students see resilience as a collective journey.
4. **Victory Collage:** Have the class assemble a "Victory Collage" using magazine cutouts, drawings, and inspirational quotes. This visual expression allows students to capture what resilience means to them, serving as a shared reminder that challenges can be stepping stones for personal growth.
5. **Grit Interviews:** Assign students to interview family members, teachers, or community members about challenges they've faced and how they overcame them. This activity provides real-life insights into resilience, adding depth to their understanding.

By engaging in these creative and reflective activities, students not only gain a deeper understanding of resilience but also learn that each setback is part of a bigger journey.

2. Teacher Strategies for Building a Resilient Classroom
While student activities foster personal reflection, teachers are uniquely positioned to create a classroom environment where

resilience flourishes. Reflect on your own experiences on the playground—each fall taught you to rise again. Now, it's our turn to pass on that lesson. Here are several strategies to help you build a resilient classroom:

1. **Be the Resilience Role Model**
   Show your students how to handle setbacks with grace. When things don't go as planned, model a calm, problem-solving approach. For instance, if a lesson isn't working as expected, share your thought process: "Looks like we need to adjust—let's do this together!"
2. **Let Failure Be a Friend, Not a Foe**
   Help students view failure as a detour to success. Create opportunities where challenges stretch their abilities—like learning to ride a bike, where a few wobbles are part of the process. Incorporate problem-solving activities and class discussions about mistakes to reinforce that every setback is a learning opportunity.
3. **Celebrate Effort, Not Just the End Result**
   Focus on the process rather than solely the final outcome. Instead of only praising a correct answer, highlight the perseverance behind the effort: "I really admire how you stuck with that, even when it got tough."
4. **Foster a Growth Mindset Culture**
   Emphasize that abilities can be developed through hard work and perseverance. Use language that celebrates growth, encourage the power of "yet," and share your own learning experiences. This helps students see that learning is an ongoing journey.
5. **Get Collaborative**
   Promote teamwork to help students learn from one another. Organize group problem-solving activities, peer feedback sessions, and partner tasks so that they can share ideas and support each other through challenges.
6. **Give Time for Reflection**
   Build in time for students to reflect on their experiences. Whether through journaling, class discussions, or exit

tickets, encourage them to consider what worked, what didn't, and how they can improve next time.
7. **Equip Them with Emotional Tools**
Teach strategies for managing emotional setbacks. Start with daily "emotion check-ins," incorporate mindfulness exercises, and help students build a "coping toolbox" with techniques like deep breathing or counting to ten when they feel overwhelmed.

When teachers model these strategies and create supportive spaces where mistakes are embraced, they empower students not only to face challenges but to learn and grow from them. Together, these student activities and teacher strategies lay a strong foundation for resilience that extends well beyond the classroom.

What Resilience Looks Like in Students

When we talk about resilient students, it's not about expecting them to never stumble or fail. In fact, resilience is built through those very struggles, and it's all about how students respond when things don't go as planned.

A truly resilient student embraces challenges rather than avoiding them. They don't see obstacles as roadblocks but as chances to grow. Whether it's a tough math problem or a new concept in class, they see it as an opportunity to learn something new, even if it feels hard at first. This mindset shift is key—they know that real growth happens when we push through the discomfort.

Another sign of resilience is the ability to ask for help. It might seem like a small thing but recognizing that reaching out for support is a strength, not a weakness, is a huge part of being resilient. When a student struggles, whether with homework or a personal issue, they aren't afraid to seek guidance. They know that learning doesn't happen in isolation, and getting help is part of the process, not something to be ashamed of.

Perseverance is another hallmark of resilience. It's about trying again and again, even when the first, second, or third attempt doesn't work out as planned. A resilient student doesn't see failure as the end; they understand it's just a part of the journey. They're willing to put in the effort, not because they're guaranteed immediate success, but because they trust that persistence will pay off over time.

Then there's self-reflection—resilient students are great at looking back and thinking about what worked, what didn't, and how they can do better next time. After a test, for example, they don't just move on to the next thing without a second thought. Instead, they review their mistakes, learn from them, and adjust their approach for next time. This ability to learn from experience makes them even stronger.

Finally, emotional regulation plays a big role. Resilient students know that it's okay to feel frustrated, disappointed, or anxious when things don't go their way. The difference is that they don't let those emotions dictate their actions. Instead, they use strategies like taking a deep breath or stepping away for a moment, knowing they'll be able to come back and tackle the problem with a clearer mind. They understand that emotions are a natural part of the process, but they don't have to control the outcome.

Building resilience is a journey, and it's something that takes time, support, and practice. But when students develop these traits, they're not just getting through challenges—they're growing stronger with everyone they face.

Final Thoughts: The Lifelong Impact of Resilience

As we've seen, resilience is more than just a reaction to failure—it's a mindset that shapes how we approach every challenge in life. Whether it's the falls and scrapes on the playground, the effort of trying again after a setback, or the courage to step up to a new challenge, resilience is what keeps us moving forward.

And the best part? It's a skill we can all cultivate, starting at a young age.

For our students, teaching resilience is about more than just bouncing back after a fall; it's about helping them recognize that growth happens when they face challenges head-on. It's about embracing the "yet"—the belief that even when they don't succeed right away, they have the ability to learn and improve. This lesson, learned on playgrounds and beyond, will serve them throughout their lives, giving them the tools they need to navigate difficulties, chase their dreams, and grow stronger with every obstacle they encounter.

As educators, we play a crucial role in nurturing this resilience. By creating a supportive environment where students can take risks, fail, learn, and keep trying, we give them the foundation for lifelong success. And by modeling resilience ourselves, we show them that even when we stumble, we too can rise, learn, and keep moving forward.

So, as you continue to guide your students, remember: every scrape, every fall, and every tough moment is an opportunity to rise stronger. Let's teach them not just to survive challenges—but to thrive because of them.

2
Rewiring Our Brains to Handle Challenges

Welcome aboard this fun and enlightening journey into the marvelous world of our brains! Today, we're going to take a trip—no stethoscope or lab coat required—to discover how our brains work and how we can help our K–5 students build resilience and success. Think of this chapter as your very own "brain-boosting" adventure, filled with engaging ideas, practical tips, and activities that make the science of neuroplasticity both accessible and fun.

Let's Take a Trip to Your Brain!

Imagine if your brain were a friend who gets startled by every little noise. You know that friend who jumps when the door creaks or overreacts to the sound of a car horn. That's kind of like our "reptilian brain"—the oldest part of our brain that's designed to protect us from danger. Back in the day, it was super useful for running from predators or dodging falling coconuts. Today, though, it sometimes overreacts to everyday challenges, like a tough math problem or a tricky social situation.

When our young students feel overwhelmed—maybe by a challenging spelling lesson or even a disagreement on the playground—their brains can switch into this fight-or-flight mode. This response floods them with stress hormones, making what should be a small bump in the road feel like a giant mountain. But don't worry! The great news is that we can help our brains (and our students' brains) learn new, more helpful ways to respond.

Rewiring Your Brain for Success: The Magic of Neuroplasticity

Here's the really cool part: our brains are incredibly flexible and can change over time. This amazing ability is called **neuroplasticity**. Think of your brain as a big lump of clay that you can shape and mold based on your experiences. Every time you practice a new skill, solve a problem or even take a deep breath during a stressful moment, you're creating new neural pathways. The more you practice, the stronger these pathways become, and the easier it is for your brain to handle challenges.

For K–5 teachers, this means you have a powerful tool in your classroom. Every time you guide your students to take a mindful breath, celebrate their effort, or reframe a mistake as a learning opportunity, you're helping to rewire their brains for resilience and success.

Survival Mode vs. Success Mode: Shifting Gears

Let's break it down with a fun metaphor. Imagine two gears in your brain:

- **Survival Mode:**
  When your brain sees a challenge, it can automatically switch to "Survival Mode." In this mode, everything feels like a crisis. Imagine a tiny math problem that suddenly

feels like an emergency! The brain floods with cortisol and adrenaline, making kids feel overwhelmed and anxious. In Survival Mode, the creative and problem-solving parts of the brain take a back seat, and it's all about protecting yourself. It's like being stuck in quicksand—frantic, frozen, and not very effective.
- **Success Mode:**
Now, picture your brain shifting into "Success Mode." In this gear, challenges are seen as opportunities. Instead of panicking, the brain says, "Okay, this is a chance to learn something new!" In Success Mode, creativity, focus, and a growth mindset take center stage. Stress turns from a roadblock into rocket fuel that helps you soar! For our students, shifting from Survival Mode to Success Mode means they learn to see mistakes as stepping stones rather than dead ends.

The key for us as teachers is to help our little learners shift gears. We can do this by modeling calm responses, teaching positive self-talk, and providing plenty of opportunities to practice problem-solving in a safe, supportive environment.

How Does Neuroplasticity Work?

Remember that our brains are like clay—malleable and ever-changing. Each time your students try something new or overcome a challenge, they're not just learning a skill—they're physically rewiring their brains. The more they practice, the stronger those new connections become. It's just like exercising a muscle: The more you use it, the stronger it gets.

Here's an everyday example: When a student struggles with tying their shoelaces, the initial frustration might trigger a fight-or-flight response. But if you encourage them to take a deep breath, try again, and eventually succeed, they're creating new neural pathways that make the task easier in the future. Over time, what once seemed impossible becomes second nature.

For young learners, simple activities—like repeated practice, playful challenges, or even mindful breathing—can lead to amazing changes in their brains. And when their brains start to see challenges as manageable, they become more resilient and ready to tackle new obstacles.

Stress: The Unexpected Ally

Let's be honest: stress doesn't always have to be the bad guy. While too much stress can be overwhelming, a little bit of stress is actually a signal that something important is happening. When managed well, stress can sharpen our focus, boost creativity, and even help us perform better. This concept is known as **stress hardiness**—the ability not just to bounce back from stress, but to grow stronger because of it.

Imagine your students are like little rockets. When stress is used correctly, it can act like fuel, propelling them forward instead of holding them back. For example, a student might feel nervous before a spelling test. Instead of freezing up, you can teach them to see that nervousness as excitement—evidence that their brain is gearing up to do something important. With practice, these small shifts in perspective can turn stress into a powerful ally rather than an obstacle.

Classroom Strategies: Shifting from Survival Mode to Success Mode

Now that we understand how our brains work and how stress can be both a challenge and an opportunity, let's talk about how to help our students shift from Survival Mode to Success Mode. Here are some simple, classroom-friendly strategies that work wonders:

1. Practice Mindfulness Together
Mindfulness isn't just for adults—it's a great way to help kids calm their brains and focus on the present moment. Try these fun, simple exercises with your students:

- **Bubble Breathing:** Ask your students to imagine they are blowing bubbles. They take a deep breath in, then slowly blow out as if they're creating the biggest, shiniest bubble ever. This playful visualization helps them slow down their breathing and calm their racing thoughts.
- **Counting Breaths:** Guide the class through a quick exercise where they count their breaths in and out. Even just one minute of mindful breathing can make a big difference when a student feels overwhelmed.

2. Encourage Positive Self-Talk

When your students say, "I can't do this" or "I'm not good at this," gently guide them to reframe their thoughts. For instance:

- Instead of "I can't do this," encourage them to say, "I haven't done this yet."
- Share fun slogans like, "Mistakes are our stepping stones!" or "Every try makes us smarter!" By practicing positive self-talk, children start to build those new neural pathways that support a growth mindset.

3. Celebrate Effort Over Outcomes

Praise your students for their hard work rather than just the results. For example, if a student struggles with a reading passage but keeps trying, celebrate their persistence. Use phrases like, "I'm so proud of how hard you worked!" or "Look at all the progress you've made!" When children learn that effort matters more than perfection, they're more willing to take on challenges and learn from their mistakes.

4. Make Physical Activity Part of the Day

Physical exercise isn't just good for the body—it's great for the brain too! Activities like stretching, dancing, or even a quick game of tag can release endorphins, helping students manage stress and stay focused. Consider:

- **Brain Breaks:** Short, energetic breaks between lessons that include simple exercises or dance routines can reset your students' stress levels and recharge their focus.

- **Mindful Movements:** Combine movement with mindfulness by having students do slow, controlled exercises like yoga poses or guided stretching.

5. Reframe Stress as a Challenge

Teach your students that stress isn't something to fear. Instead, help them see it as a challenge they can overcome. You might say, "This problem might feel tough right now, but every challenge helps our brain grow stronger!" Use stories and examples—like how a superhero faces obstacles—to illustrate that challenges are just opportunities in disguise.

Rewiring Activities for the Classroom

Let's bring all of these ideas to life with some engaging, hands-on activities that are perfect for K–5 classrooms. These activities are designed to help students practice rewiring their brains in fun, memorable ways.

Activity 1: Mindfulness Breathing Exercise

Objective: Calm the mind and activate the "Success Mode" of the brain.

How to Do It:

1. Gather the students in a circle or have them sit quietly at their desks.
2. Explain that you're going to do a "bubble breathing" exercise.
3. Instruct them to take a deep breath in slowly for a count of four, imagine they're filling a big bubble, hold the breath for four counts, and then exhale slowly for four counts, as if the bubble is floating away.
4. Repeat this exercise three to five times.
5. Discuss briefly how they felt before and after the exercise.

Teacher Tip: Use a visual aid like a picture of a bubble or even a fun, short video that explains bubble breathing in a child-friendly way.

Activity 2: Growth Mindset Reflection Journal
Objective: Help students reflect on challenges and recognize their growth.
How to Do It:

1. Provide each student with a simple journal or a few sheets of paper stapled together.
2. Offer prompts such as:
    - "Write or draw about a time when something was hard, but you kept trying."
    - "What did you learn from that challenge?"
    - "How did it make you feel when you finally solved it?"
3. Allow students some quiet time at the end of the day or week to complete their reflections.
4. Encourage sharing in small groups or as a class (voluntarily) to build a supportive community.

Teacher Tip: Emphasize that there are no right or wrong answers—this journal is just for them to see how they're growing.

Activity 3: Resilience Role Play
Objective: Practice handling challenges through creative, supportive role play.

How to Do It:

1. Prepare a few simple scenarios on cards (e.g., "You forgot your homework," "You had a disagreement with a friend," "You didn't understand a class activity").
2. Divide the class into small groups and give each group a scenario.
3. Ask the groups to act out the situation, then come up with different ways to respond.
4. After each role play, have a brief discussion about which responses helped shift the situation from a stress reaction to a success response.
5. Highlight strategies such as taking a deep breath, using positive self-talk, or asking for help.

Teacher Tip: Model one scenario first to show students how role play can be a safe space for experimenting with new ideas.

Activity 4: The Resilience Relay

Objective: Combine physical activity with teamwork and problem-solving to reinforce the idea that challenges build strength.

How to Do It:

1. Set up a simple obstacle course or relay race in the classroom or outside.
2. Each station in the relay includes a small challenge—such as solving a simple puzzle, doing a quick stretch, or reciting a positive phrase.
3. Students work in teams to complete the course.
4. After the relay, have a group discussion about how working together helped overcome the challenges and made everyone feel stronger.

Teacher Tip: Adapt the relay to suit your space and available resources. The key is to ensure it's fun and non-competitive, focusing on teamwork and perseverance.

A Story of Transformation: From Struggle to Success

Let's bring these ideas to life with a real-life story. Meet Jake, a second-grader who once found reading to be a huge challenge. Every time Jake faced a difficult word, his frustration would skyrocket, and he'd feel like giving up. His teacher noticed that Jake's brain was stuck in Survival Mode—his stress response was taking over every time he encountered something tough.

Then, Jake's teacher introduced a series of small, consistent strategies: daily mindfulness breathing exercises, a fun growth mindset journal where he could draw his feelings, and regular role-playing activities where he learned that mistakes were just stepping stones. Slowly but surely, Jake began to shift from feeling overwhelmed to feeling excited about challenges. His teachers and classmates noticed the change—Jake started to smile more, ask questions, and even volunteer to read aloud. Today, Jake isn't just reading with more confidence; he's become a role model for resilience in his class.

Stories like Jake's remind us that when we rewire our brains through positive experiences and supportive practices, the transformation is nothing short of amazing.

Practical Tips for K–5 Teachers to Foster Brain Rewiring

Before we wrap up, here are some quick, teacher-friendly tips to integrate these concepts into your daily routine:

- **Be a Role Model:** Show your students that you, too, use strategies like deep breathing and positive self-talk. Share a quick story of when you felt challenged and how you overcame it.
- **Keep It Light and Playful:** Use humor and fun analogies (like our friend who jumps at every noise!) to explain complex concepts in a simple way.
- **Celebrate Every Effort:** Create a classroom culture where every attempt is celebrated. Use stickers, high-fives, or a "Resilience Star" chart to recognize progress.
- **Make It Routine:** Incorporate a brief mindfulness or reflection session into the daily schedule. Consistency helps these new neural pathways strengthen over time.
- **Encourage Peer Support:** Pair students up for activities like role play or the resilience relay. When kids see their friends overcoming challenges, it builds a shared culture of growth and resilience.
- **Use Visual Aids:** Charts, posters, and simple diagrams that illustrate "Survival Mode" vs. "Success Mode" can be a constant, gentle reminder of the growth mindset you're nurturing in your classroom.

- **Communicate with Families:** Send home a simple newsletter or a handout that explains these strategies. When parents understand what you're doing in class, they can reinforce these habits at home.

Final Thoughts: The Power of Small Shifts, Big Changes

Rewiring the brain for resilience is not about making huge leaps overnight—it's about embracing small, consistent shifts that add up over time. Every mindful breath, every bit of positive self-talk, and every shared success story is a tiny brick in the foundation of a resilient, adaptable mind. As K–5 educators, you are in a unique position to plant these seeds of growth in your students at a very formative age.

Remember, the goal isn't to eliminate stress completely but to help our students see it as a signal—a call to action to rise to the challenge. With each small shift, their brains grow stronger, more flexible, and more capable of turning obstacles into opportunities. And the beauty of neuroplasticity is that it works for everyone—teachers and students alike.

So, as you step into your classroom each day, know that you're not just teaching reading, math, or science—you're nurturing resilient minds that will carry the power of these small shifts into every challenge they face in life.

Together, let's celebrate the journey of rewiring our brains and our hearts. Let's turn stress from a foe into a friend, transform every struggle into a learning moment, and create a classroom where every child believes that they have the power to succeed, no matter what.

Here's to a future filled with curious minds, brave hearts, and resilient spirits—one mindful breath at a time!

3

Teaching "Not Yet" and Growth Mindset

Imagine a baby learning to walk. They wobble, they tumble, and without missing a beat, they get right back up to try again. That's pure resilience in action! And when we talk about a baby's progress, we don't ask, "Are they walking?" We ask, "Are they walking yet?" Because we know they will. We never question their ability to eventually succeed—we trust the process. No one tells a baby, "Maybe walking just isn't for you." We instinctively understand that they won't give up until they master the skill.

But somewhere along the way, as we grow up, that mindset fades. We start to believe that failure is final. We hesitate, doubt ourselves, and sometimes even stop trying altogether. The truth is that children are actually born with a natural level of resilience. Unlike adults, they haven't yet been conditioned to fear failure the way they will be in school, where mistakes are often penalized rather than seen as stepping stones to success. What if we could preserve that resilience? What if we could reshape the way students see learning—not as a series of tests they either pass or fail, but as a journey of continual growth?

As adults, we've forgotten what it's like to not know something. We often assume we should be good at things right away. And as teachers, we sometimes expect students to come equipped with confidence and perseverance. But just like babies learning to walk, students take their first steps in learning with uncertainty, and sometimes they fall. Our job is to remind them that stumbling is not a sign of failure—it's a sign of progress.

Now, let's pause here. Yet is not just a word. It's the magic word—the word that transforms failure into growth, impossible into possible, and limits into obstacles waiting to be overcome. When a student says, "I can't do this," we can help them reframe it: "I can't do this… yet." That one simple shift changes everything. It creates room for patience, persistence, and the belief that ability is not fixed but developed.

So, the next time a student struggles, remind them: success isn't about being perfect the first time—it's about persistence. The only difference between I can't, and I can is yet. And with that one word, we give them permission to keep going, to keep learning, and to trust that they, too, will walk forward—one step at a time.

The Magic Word: Yet

Okay, let's talk about yet—the little word that packs a punch. It's one of those words you don't always give a second thought to, but when you do, it's like you're unlocking a treasure chest of potential. Adding "I can't do it" doesn't just keep it at "I can't" — it transforms it into a hopeful promise: "I can't do it yet." It's an invitation to press on, to keep trying, and to trust that growth is always just around the corner.

When a student is struggling with math, and you say, "I know this feels tough, but you can't do it yet," that's more than just reassurance—it's a mindset shift. It's telling them, "You're not failing; you're learning. You're not stuck; you're on the path to figuring it out." They're not bound by limitations; they're bound for growth.

Tip for K-5: Turn yet into a classroom habit. Set up a "Yet Wall" where students can share things they can't do yet, like "I can't read chapter books yet" or "I can't do multiplication yet." Celebrate those little victories and progress, adding new examples as they go. It shows them that struggling isn't the same as failing—it's part of the learning process.

Now, here's a fun idea: What if you wore a yet badge every day? It could be literal, or just a mental reminder that where you are now is just a snapshot, and tomorrow holds endless possibilities. Imagine how much more exciting learning could be if we—and our students—embraced the power of yet in everything we do. It's not just a word. It's a mindset, and it's absolutely magical.

What's Happening in Our Classrooms?

As young learners, children are naturally curious. They love to explore, experiment, and figure out how things work. If they can't do something, they don't give up—they try again and again, like little explorers on a grand adventure. But then, something changes. As children get older, they start to feel pressure from school. Grades, tests, assignments—suddenly, learning becomes about proving you're good enough instead of figuring things out. Mistakes, which were once part of the fun, start to feel like failures to avoid. And before long, students stop seeing mistakes as opportunities to learn and instead view them as roadblocks to their success.

This shift in mindset doesn't happen overnight. It's the result of the pressure to perform, to be perfect, and to always succeed on the first try. Students start fearing failure, fearing mistakes. But here's the thing: mistakes are the best part of learning! When we try something new, we don't always get it right at first. That's normal. In fact, it's essential. But if we can teach our students to see mistakes as part of the process, we open up a whole new world for them.

That's where the word yet comes in. It's a subtle but powerful change in how we view challenges. Instead of seeing them as walls, we see them as ladders. Instead of "I can't do it," we say, "I can't do it yet." It's not just about getting to the end—it's about enjoying the process.

Growth Mindset vs. Fixed Mindset

When it comes to shaping the way students approach challenges, one of the most influential theories is Carol Dweck's concept of *mindset*. According to Dweck, people operate under one of two primary mindsets: **Growth Mindset** and **Fixed Mindset**. These mindsets dictate how we perceive our abilities and how we respond to challenges, effort, and setbacks. Dweck's groundbreaking research has shown that how students view their intelligence and abilities can have a profound impact on their academic success, resilience, and overall development.

- **Growth Mindset:** A growth mindset is the belief that intelligence, skills, and abilities can be developed through effort, learning, and persistence. Students with a growth mindset see challenges as opportunities to learn rather than obstacles to avoid. They believe that failure is not a reflection of their abilities, but a necessary part of the learning process. The "yet" mindset perfectly aligns with this view. When a student says, "I can't do this yet," they are embracing the idea that their ability to succeed is a matter of perseverance and practice, not something fixed from birth.
- **Fixed Mindset:** In contrast, a fixed mindset is the belief that intelligence and abilities are static traits, something you are either born with or you are not. Students with a fixed mindset view failure as evidence that they aren't "smart enough" or "good enough," and they may avoid challenges to protect themselves from making mistakes. They tend to give up easily when faced with difficulty and might believe that talent alone is what leads to success. They might say, "I can't do this," and leave it at that, without the hope of improvement.

Dweck's Research and Impact
Carol Dweck's research, particularly in her seminal work *Mindset: The New Psychology of Success* (2006), has shown that

students who adopt a growth mindset are more likely to persist through challenges, embrace effort as part of learning, and ultimately achieve greater success. Dweck's studies reveal that **praising effort rather than innate ability** can lead students to adopt a growth mindset and become more resilient in the face of setbacks.

For instance, in her study with fifth graders, Dweck and her colleagues found that students who were praised for their effort, rather than their innate intelligence, showed a greater willingness to take on challenges and were more likely to perform better in the long run. They learned to view their abilities as something they could cultivate over time. This aligns directly with the concept of "yet"—the understanding that abilities are not permanent and can be developed with practice.

Applying the Growth Mindset in the Classroom

In the classroom, adopting a growth mindset approach transforms the way we engage with students, particularly when it comes to struggles and setbacks. Instead of focusing on outcomes, the focus shifts to the process—the effort, the perseverance, and the learning journey. This shift from outcome-based thinking to process-based thinking is a fundamental aspect of fostering a growth mindset.

By using the word "yet," we make it clear that a student's current struggle is not an indication of their permanent limitations. Instead of telling a student, "This is too hard for you," a teacher with a growth mindset would say, "You haven't mastered this *yet*, but with practice, you will get there." This creates a safe space for failure, where mistakes are seen as opportunities to learn and grow, rather than as signs of inadequacy.

The power of *yet* doesn't just stop with students—it applies to teachers as well. Teachers who have a growth mindset are more likely to continue learning and improving their own practices, taking risks in their teaching, and embracing new challenges. Just like students, teachers benefit from viewing challenges as part of a larger, ongoing learning process.

Further Implications of Growth Mindset

Dweck's work extends beyond just academic success; it also influences personal development and social relationships. Students with a growth mindset tend to have better coping skills, as they view challenges as a natural part of life. This mindset fosters emotional resilience, where setbacks are less likely to lead to feelings of helplessness or depression.

Research supports this notion, demonstrating that a growth mindset encourages adaptive coping strategies, such as problem-solving and seeking help, rather than maladaptive behaviors like avoidance or giving up. By reinforcing the idea that abilities can be developed and improved over time, students with a growth mindset are better equipped to handle stress and overcome obstacles in their academic and personal lives.

How to Foster a Growth Mindset: Classroom Strategies

To encourage a growth mindset in the classroom, here are a few strategies that research suggests are effective:

1. **Praise Effort, Not Innate Ability:** As Dweck's research has shown, praising effort and perseverance is far more effective in cultivating a growth mindset than praising intelligence or natural ability. Instead of saying, "You're so smart," say things like, "You worked really hard on this, and it's paying off."
2. **Emphasize Learning Over Performance:** Focus on the learning process rather than the final result. When a student encounters difficulty, remind them that the struggle is part of growth. Emphasize that mastering a difficult concept is a process that takes time, and mistakes are just stepping stones along the way.
3. **Model a Growth Mindset:** Teachers can demonstrate a growth mindset by showing how they, too, face

challenges and learn from them. For example, teachers can say things like, "I don't know the answer to this yet, but I'm going to work through it and figure it out."
4. **Use the Word "Yet:"** Encourage students to say "yet" when they face a challenge. Instead of saying, "I can't do this," encourage them to say, "I can't do this yet," to remind them that success is a matter of persistence.
5. **Create a "Fail Forward" Environment:** Normalize mistakes as part of the learning process. Encourage students to reflect on their mistakes and learn from them, rather than viewing mistakes as failures. When students embrace mistakes as part of the growth process, they become more willing to take risks and try new things.

Final Thoughts: Fun Strategies to Bring the Power of "Yet" into Your Classroom

Ready to turn your classroom into a place where mistakes are celebrated, growth is encouraged, and every "I can't" is followed by "yet"? Here are some additional, fun strategies to help make yet a central part of your teaching toolkit:

Cheer on Effort, Not Just Results

It's easy to fall into the trap of focusing solely on results, but **celebrating the effort** that goes into learning is just as important, especially for children. Some people argue that we should only cheer results and not effort, believing that praising effort without acknowledging the outcome could create a false sense of accomplishment. However, this perspective overlooks a fundamental aspect of how learning works, particularly for children.

Remember the baby learning to walk, well what if we only cheered for perfect walking, the baby might never even try to take those first steps! We celebrate their effort and progress because we understand that learning to walk is a process—there will be tumbles and mistakes, but those are essential parts of growth.

The same applies to students in the classroom. When children are trying new things—whether it's solving a tough math problem, learning a new instrument, or trying a new sport—they are often outside their comfort zone. If we only celebrate when things go perfectly, we risk discouraging them from trying again. When we cheer their effort, we send the message that it's the *process* that matters just as much as the end result.

Critics of effort-based praise often argue that it can lead to complacency or a lack of drive. But this criticism is misguided. Praising effort isn't about dismissing results; it's about helping students understand that **growth** is a gradual process. Mistakes are inevitable, and learning happens through persistence. In fact, the research is clear that fostering a growth mindset in children is far more beneficial in the long run than simply applauding perfect outcomes.

Instead of simply saying, "Great job!" try saying something like, "I love how hard you're working on this—it's not perfect yet, but you're making great progress!" This kind of praise encourages students to focus on their development rather than just the final result. It helps them see that their efforts, persistence, and determination are what matter most. And just as importantly, it helps them view challenges as opportunities rather than as threats to their self-esteem.

When students are regularly praised for their efforts, they develop a mindset that values the journey over the destination. This shifts their focus from being "right" to being resilient and *persistent*. In turn, they become more open to taking risks, more willing to face challenges, and more likely to persevere in the face of adversity. This is exactly what we want for our students, both in school and in life: the ability to keep going, even when the path isn't easy.

For adults to expect students to focus only on results and not appreciate effort is just as misguided as expecting a baby to walk perfectly the first time. If we don't cheer on a child's effort, we risk undermining their confidence and creating a fear of failure that stifles learning. The reality is that growth is messy, and so is the learning process. It's essential that we support students by celebrating their progress, hard work, and resilience, not just the final product, is what truly matters, it shifts their focus from being "right" to being resilient.

1. **Make Risk-Taking Fun and Safe**
   Help your students understand that taking risks is part of the learning process by sharing your own funny stories of mistakes and failures. Whether it's a time you tried something new in the classroom that didn't work out quite right, or a personal experience where you stumbled before succeeding—let them see that failure isn't something to fear. By normalizing mistakes, you create a classroom culture where students feel safe to take risks, knowing they can learn from every misstep. When students are encouraged to fail forward, they begin to embrace "yet" as their trusted ally in the learning process.

2. **Incorporate "Yet" in Everyday Conversations**
   Get creative with how you use yet in your conversations. When a student says, "I can't do it," gently remind them to add the magic word: "You can't do it yet, but you're on the right path!" It's a small shift in language, but it reinforces the powerful idea that success isn't instant—it's a process. The more often students hear the word yet, the more they begin to internalize the belief that they can improve, learn, and grow with time and effort. This simple act transforms each challenge into a potential victory.

3. **Use Visual Reminders**
   Create a classroom bulletin board or poster that says, "I can't do it yet!" with student-friendly illustrations and examples. Whenever a student expresses doubt or frustration, direct them to this visual reminder. It helps them connect their feelings with the bigger picture—that learning is a journey, and struggles are part of the process. The more you reinforce this message, the more your students will start to see setbacks as opportunities to grow.

4. **Turn Struggles into Success Stories**
   When a student overcomes a challenge after initially struggling, celebrate it as a success story. Share these

moments with the class, highlighting the progress made. These moments show students that it's not about being perfect from the start—it's about how we keep going, keep trying, and keep learning. By turning struggles into success stories, you make every mistake and every challenge a vital part of the success journey.

4
Tapping into Students' Unique Strengths

Ah, the classroom—the place where every day is an adventure. Some days are smooth sailing, and other days… well, let's just say you might need a parachute. But if there's one thing I've learned, it's that the most powerful growth often sprouts from the students who face the toughest challenges.

At first, like many teachers, I thought success was all about the students who aced every test, breezed through assignments, and looked like they had life figured out. You know, the "perfect" students. But guess what? I soon realized that the true mark of success isn't about perfection—it's about resilience. It's about being able to stumble, fall, pick yourself back up, and keep going with an even greater determination than before. It's that inner strength that no textbook can teach—that's what leads to real success.

When I first stepped into the classroom, I focused heavily on academic achievement. If a student got an A+? Victory! But after a while, I discovered something much more profound—it's not the straight-A students who teach us the most; it's the ones who struggle, fall, and get back up again. Those are the students who have the potential to rise and soar higher than anyone imagined.

Resilience: The Secret Sauce for Real Success

Now, let's clear something up about resilience—it's not just about bouncing back from failure. Oh no! It's about developing the mental and emotional muscle to tackle challenges head-on. It's about flipping failure on its head and saying, "Nice try, but I'm coming back stronger!" When we nurture resilience in our students, we're giving them the power to not just survive school but to thrive through it.

But how do we help our students develop that kind of resilience? Easy! By focusing on their strengths. Yup, you read that right. It's all about turning what they're good at into their superpower.

The Magic of Strength-Based Learning: Unlocking Resilience in Every Student

Let me rewind for a second. Back when I started teaching life science, I was knee-deep in grades, tests, and the never-ending cycle of academic "success." Sure, students were doing well on their tests, but they weren't fully engaged. They were just going through the motions. That's when I had my "Aha!" moment. What if I looked beyond the grades and focused on what students were actually good at? And not just in science, but in life?

Enter: outdoor team-building activities. I took my class outside, where things got a little less "academic" and a lot more adventurous. As a certified ropes course facilitator, I introduced my students to challenges that required teamwork, trust, and—yep, you guessed it—resilience. Suddenly, I was seeing sides of my students I never knew existed.

One day, a student who was known for struggling with science became the hero of the day. The ropes course had an obstacle that seemed impossible. His team was stuck, completely unsure how to get through it. But guess who stepped up and took charge? This student! He became an unexpected leader, guiding his team through the challenge and helping them succeed. He wasn't the top student in science, but that moment of triumph gave him a huge boost in confidence.

And then, there was the quiet student—who would barely speak up in class—leading her team with the kind of precision and confidence that made me do a double-take. It was like seeing a whole new version of her. That outdoor experience unleashed her leadership, and just like that, her self-esteem skyrocketed.

By focusing on their strengths, I was helping them build resilience in ways I had never imagined.

The Resilience Formula: Strengths + Success = Confidence

As educators, we often focus so much on student weaknesses—what they don't do well, where they fall short—that we forget about what truly builds their inner resilience. So many students walk into school each day with a fear of failure because they rarely experience success. They become conditioned to see themselves as incapable, and they start to doubt whether they can succeed at all.

But what if we flipped that? What if, instead of solely focusing on what students can't do, we centered our teaching around their strengths and celebrated every small success? The Resilience Formula I created is grounded in this idea: **Strengths + Success = Confidence**. When students experience success and realize that they are capable, that's when they truly start to build resilience. It's not just about bouncing back from setbacks; it's about forging an unshakable belief in themselves that propels them forward.

This formula isn't just theoretical—it's transformative. I've seen firsthand how this approach not only elevates student performance but fosters a mindset that allows them to take on challenges with confidence. Let's break down the formula and explore how each step builds on the last to help students develop the resilience they need to thrive, no matter the circumstances.

Step 1: Unleashing Potential Through Strengths

Strengths are the foundation of resilience. Every student has something they do well—whether it's solving a problem creatively, leading a team, or simply showing empathy for their peers. The challenge is helping students see those strengths. Too often, students focus on their weaknesses, and as educators, we often emphasize areas that need improvement. While growth is important, it must begin with recognizing and celebrating what students *already* do well.

Why this step matters: By identifying and building on their strengths, students gain a sense of self-worth and see the value they bring to the classroom. When we start from their strengths, it creates a positive foundation that encourages them to take risks and move beyond their comfort zone.

Strategy Tip: Use tools like strength-based assessments or encourage students to reflect on their personal successes. Create a classroom culture that celebrates small wins. This gives students a chance to shine, and as they do, they begin to realize their potential.

Example: One of my students excelled at art, but she struggled with writing assignments. By allowing her to use her creativity in illustrating her writing projects, her confidence grew. She didn't just succeed in art; she applied her newfound confidence to her written work, and soon her writing was improving too.

Step 2: Success Through Strengths

Once students recognize their strengths, we must give them opportunities to experience success by leveraging those strengths. This is the point where students see that success isn't about being perfect in everything—it's about finding what they're good at and using it to achieve goals.

Why this step matters: Success reinforces the belief that they *can* succeed, especially when they use their unique abilities. When students experience success, it's not just a feel-good moment—it becomes proof that they are capable. This success feeds into their confidence, reinforcing that they *can* achieve more.

Strategy Tip: Allow students to take the lead in activities that align with their strengths. When they succeed using their own abilities, it's a powerful reinforcement of their self-worth and potential. Celebrate these moments, big or small, to help them build resilience.

Example: A student who struggled with math but excelled in collaborative tasks was given a leadership role in a group project. By succeeding in guiding his peers, his confidence in himself soared, and he started applying that confidence in other subjects, like math.

Step 3: Building Confidence Through Success

The key to resilience is confidence. Confidence doesn't come from winning every time—it comes from knowing that you have the strength to try, fail, and try again. When students experience success and are celebrated for it, they begin to internalize the belief that they *can* face challenges. They don't have to be perfect—they just need to believe in themselves and their ability to handle whatever comes next.

Why this step matters: Confidence is the fuel for continued success. It enables students to trust themselves and their abilities, helping them push through challenges with the knowledge that failure isn't the end—it's part of the journey. When students feel confident, they're more likely to embrace future challenges and continue growing.

Strategy Tip: Be specific and intentional with praise. Recognize the effort, creativity, or collaboration that led to their success. This isn't about making students feel good for the sake of it; it's about reinforcing the qualities that made their success possible so they can replicate it in the future.

Example: One of my students, who struggled with self-doubt, was praised for his exceptional problem-solving skills during a class project. This recognition built his confidence, and the next time a challenge arose, he was eager to tackle it head-on, applying his newly reinforced self-belief.

Step 4: Embracing New Challenges

Once students have experienced success and built confidence, they become more willing to try new things, take on harder challenges, and even fail. Why? Because they now understand that failure isn't the end of the road—it's part of the growth process. With their foundation of success, they've learned that they can overcome obstacles and that they have the strength to keep going, no matter the outcome.

Why this step matters: Students who have experienced success are more likely to tackle difficult tasks, knowing they can handle the challenges ahead. When failure does come (as it inevitably will), it doesn't crush their confidence—it motivates them to try again. It's in this cycle of challenge, success, and learning from failure that resilience truly takes root.

Strategy Tip: Encourage students to set stretch goals that are slightly outside their comfort zone. Normalize failure as a natural part of growth and help students reflect on what they've learned from setbacks. This helps them see that every challenge, no matter the outcome, is an opportunity for growth.

Example: A student who had a fear of public speaking gained confidence by succeeding in small group presentations. Over time, this success made him willing to take on larger audiences, and when he faltered, it didn't shake his confidence. He simply adjusted, learned, and kept trying.

Step 5: Resilient Growth

Resilience isn't just about bouncing back—it's about becoming stronger each time you face a challenge. Once students experience a series of successes and failures, they begin to see resilience as part of their identity. With each new challenge, they become more confident in their ability to succeed, and they're less afraid to fail because they've learned that failure is not the end—it's part of the process.

Why this step matters: Resilience is not a destination—it's a journey. The more students practice resilience, the more ingrained it becomes. This mindset shift helps them tackle any challenge with the belief that they can persevere.

Strategy Tip: Continually reinforce the idea that resilience is a skill that can be developed over time. Encourage students to reflect on their growth and how far they've come, not just in academic success but in overcoming life's obstacles. This reinforces their belief in themselves.

Example: At the end of each term, I have students reflect on how they've faced challenges and what they've learned along the way. This helps them see how resilience is built step by step and empowers them to continue growing.

Tapping Into Resilience Through Strengths

In the classroom, resilience isn't just a nice-to-have trait—it's the very foundation of success. It's not about avoiding failure but about how we respond to it. The students who stumble and fall, the ones who struggle and get back up again, are often the ones who surprise us with their growth and potential. They are the ones who teach us that real success is not defined by perfection but by perseverance.

Through the years, I've learned that the key to unlocking true resilience in students lies not in fixing their weaknesses but in recognizing and amplifying their strengths. These strengths aren't just academic—they are human qualities that, when nurtured, can transform how students view themselves and the world around them.

When we shift our focus from what students can't do to what they *can* do, we empower them to see their own potential. This is where resilience begins—by acknowledging that every student has the ability to rise above challenges, not in spite of their struggles but because of them.

The classroom becomes a place where students no longer fear failure but embrace it as a stepping stone to growth. They don't just survive—they thrive, armed with the confidence that comes from knowing they are capable, valued, and supported.

Final Thoughts: Strength and Success

By connecting students' strengths to their success, we nurture a deeper sense of confidence, which fuels their resilience. It's not just about teaching them how to overcome setbacks; it's about teaching them to see setbacks as opportunities to grow stronger, more determined, and more self-assured.

This isn't a one-time fix—it's an ongoing process, one that requires our continued commitment to cultivating an environment of trust, encouragement, and opportunity. Every time a student rises to a challenge, we take another step toward creating a culture of resilience. One success, one challenge, and one relationship at a time.

When we focus on their strengths and build their resilience, we're not just preparing students for academic success. We're preparing them for life. And that's the real legacy we leave behind: students who understand that they are capable of facing any obstacle because they've learned to rise again, stronger each time.

Resilience isn't a trait that some students are born with—it's a skill that can be cultivated, nurtured, and passed on. And as educators, we are in the best position to teach them how to tap into it.

Let's keep fostering that growth, one strength at a time.

5
Fostering Emotional Awareness and Intelligence

Why It's Okay for Students to Feel Bad—and How They Can Use Those Feelings

Imagine you're in your classroom, and little Johnny just lost the class spelling bee. His face is scrunched up, tears are welling, and he's on the brink of a meltdown. Instead of seeing this as a disaster, what if we viewed it as a golden opportunity to teach Johnny about his emotions?

We've all heard Maya Angelou's famous words: "They may forget what you said — but they will never forget how you made them feel." This isn't just a catchy quote; it's a reminder that our emotional interactions with students leave lasting impressions.

Maya Angelou herself faced numerous challenges, from early trauma to struggles with self-worth. Yet, she blossomed into a celebrated writer and teacher who deeply understood the power of emotional connections. She believed that resilience isn't just about overcoming external hurdles but also about developing the emotional strength to grow amidst adversity.

For us educators, the takeaway is clear: Creating a classroom environment where students feel valued and understood is as crucial as any academic lesson. When students feel safe and emotionally supported, they're better equipped to navigate difficulties and build resilience. Angelou (2008) often said, "You may not control all the events that happen to you, but you can decide not to be reduced by them." This mindset encourages students to view challenges not as insurmountable barriers but as opportunities for growth.

By making our students feel seen and supported, we help them develop the emotional intelligence necessary to handle life's ups and downs with confidence. While they may forget the specifics of our lessons, they'll always remember the emotional connection and the belief we instilled in their ability to overcome challenges.

Emotional Intelligence: A Strength, Not the Enemy

Emotional intelligence (EQ) is often misunderstood, especially in educational settings. Teachers and students alike are frequently told that emotions must be controlled, repressed, or ignored in order to focus on academic achievement. However, the reality is quite the opposite: Emotions, when understood and managed, can be a powerful tool for growth, learning, and resilience.

So, what exactly is EQ?

At its core, emotional intelligence is about recognizing, understanding, and managing your own emotions, while also being able to recognize, understand, and influence the emotions of others. It's a mix of self-awareness, self-regulation, empathy, and social skills. When we talk about success, we usually hear a lot about IQ (Intelligence Quotient), but research shows that EQ plays an equally, if not more, important role in determining a person's success, happiness, and overall well-being.

For students, emotional intelligence helps them navigate social dynamics, stay focused on tasks, bounce back from setbacks, and adapt to new challenges. These skills aren't just "nice to have"—they're essential for thriving in school and beyond.

The Power of Self-Awareness in Students

One of the most important aspects of EQ is self-awareness—the ability to recognize your emotions and their impact. Imagine this: a student named Sarah feels frustrated after struggling with a math problem. Instead of letting her frustration build into full-blown anxiety, Sarah pauses and thinks, "Okay, I'm frustrated right now. I can feel my heart racing, and my face is getting hot. It's okay to feel this way, but I need to take a deep breath and think about the next step."

In this moment, Sarah's self-awareness allows her to stop the emotional spiral. She becomes mindful of her feelings, instead of being controlled by them. This ability to observe and understand her emotions empowers Sarah to make more rational decisions, stay calm under pressure, and avoid making rash decisions. Self-awareness builds resilience, helping students manage difficult emotions without letting them control their actions or thoughts.

When students understand their emotional responses, they can start using their feelings as tools rather than obstacles. It's about acknowledging what they feel without allowing it to dominate their behavior. This proactive approach to emotions helps students grow stronger in the face of difficulty.

The Role of Self-Regulation in Building Resilience

Self-regulation is another critical part of emotional intelligence. It's the ability to manage one's emotions in a healthy way, control impulses, and remain focused—even in tough situations. Self-regulation allows us to choose how we respond to our emotions, rather than just reacting without thinking.

Imagine a student named David, who's about to take a big test. He feels nervous and anxious, which could cause him to freeze up or rush through the test without thinking clearly. But David has developed self-regulation skills. Instead of letting his anxiety dictate his actions, he chooses to pause, take deep breaths, and remind himself that he's prepared and capable.

Self-regulation helps students stay calm in challenging situations, make thoughtful decisions, and maintain their focus. The ability to manage stress and stay on track, even when faced with anxiety, is a huge advantage—both academically and in life.

Empathy: The Bridge to Connection

Empathy is one of the most powerful components of EQ. It's the ability to understand and share the feelings of others, and it's essential for building positive relationships. When students are empathetic, they can see things from other people's perspectives and respond with kindness and care.

For example, Elena notices that her classmate Marco is upset after getting a low grade. Instead of ignoring him or assuming he'll "get over it," Elena approaches Marco and asks if he's okay. By recognizing his feelings and offering support, Elena demonstrates empathy.

Empathy is a superpower that fosters cooperation, reduces conflict, and creates a positive classroom environment. When students feel understood and supported, they're more likely to engage in learning and contribute to a positive school culture.

Why EQ Is a Strength

When students develop emotional intelligence (EQ), they're not just learning to control or suppress their emotions; they're discovering how to channel their emotions as strengths. EQ empowers them to turn every emotional experience into an opportunity for growth and learning. For example, when students encounter stress or frustration, they're able to recognize these emotions and use them as signals to adjust their approach or mindset. Instead of letting negative emotions hinder progress, EQ enables students to persevere and reframe challenges as learning opportunities.

Emotional intelligence equips students with essential tools for navigating the complexities of everyday life. Whether it's managing peer relationships, dealing with academic pressures, or facing personal challenges, emotionally intelligent students have a better understanding of their emotional states. This self-awareness allows them to make informed choices about how to respond, and, in turn, helps them build stronger connections with others. As a result, EQ isn't just about overcoming difficulties; it's about developing resilience, adaptability, and the emotional flexibility needed to succeed in all areas of life.

Building EQ for Long-Term Success

For educators, fostering emotional intelligence in students isn't just a short-term goal—it's an investment in their long-term success. Creating an environment where emotional intelligence can thrive involves more than just teaching techniques; it requires modeling EQ, offering support, and providing opportunities for practice.

- **Model Emotional Intelligence**: Teachers are powerful role models. When educators demonstrate emotional intelligence by managing their own emotions, staying calm in high-pressure situations, and practicing empathy, they set the tone for students to follow. This modeling is crucial because students learn best when they can see EQ in action. It also teaches them that emotions are not something to be feared or suppressed, but something to understand and work with.
- **Create Safe Spaces for Emotional Expression**: In a classroom that encourages emotional intelligence, students should feel comfortable expressing how they feel, knowing that their emotions are valid and respected. This safe environment helps students understand that emotions are natural and part of the human experience. Whether it's joy, anger, sadness, or fear, students need to know they can express their feelings without judgment. This encourages emotional authenticity and builds trust within the classroom community.
- **Promote Problem-Solving**: Teaching students emotional regulation techniques is a key aspect of building emotional resilience. Methods such as deep breathing,

journaling, and mindfulness exercises can help students manage their emotions more effectively. By teaching students how to pause, reflect, and respond, we give them the tools to overcome emotional hurdles without letting their feelings take over. Over time, these techniques can become second nature, helping students navigate challenges with emotional maturity and resilience.

By focusing on emotional intelligence, we're not just helping students succeed in school—we're helping them build the foundation for success in life. EQ equips them with the skills needed to manage relationships, adapt to changing circumstances, and thrive in both their personal and professional lives. In a world that is constantly changing and often stressful, emotionally intelligent individuals are better able to stay grounded, confident, and capable of facing whatever comes their way.

Actionable Tip: The Five-Minute Emotional Reset

This simple exercise helps students break free from negative emotional cycles and reset their mindset. It's a quick yet powerful technique for students to regain control over their emotions and refocus on positive action.

1. **Name the Emotion**: Have students identify what they're feeling (e.g., "I'm frustrated, and that's okay"). This step encourages self-awareness and helps students differentiate between emotions, which is the first step in managing them.
2. **Accept It Without Judgment**: Remind them that it's completely normal to experience negative emotions. Teach students that acknowledging their feelings without judgment allows them to move through the emotion instead of suppressing it, which is a critical skill for emotional regulation.

3. **Reflect with Self-Aware Questions**:

   ♦ What triggered this emotion? This helps students identify external and internal factors contributing to their feelings.
   ♦ How is this emotion affecting my behavior? Encourages reflection on how emotions influence actions and decisions.
   ♦ What can I learn from this experience? Shifts the focus from feeling bad to seeing the situation as a learning opportunity.
4. **Let It Pass**: Help students recognize that emotions are temporary and will pass with time. Remind them that they have the power to change their emotional state through conscious action.
5. **Redirect Focus**: Ask students, "What action can I take now to move forward?" This helps students shift from a negative emotional state to a positive, solution-oriented mindset. This is crucial for developing emotional resilience—by taking proactive steps, students learn to move past emotions and focus on constructive outcomes.

This exercise helps students not only manage emotions but also build resilience by transforming negative feelings into opportunities for self-growth and forward momentum.

Turning Emotions into Rocket Fuel for Resilience

Often, we view emotions like frustration, disappointment, or sadness as obstacles to overcome. But what if we viewed these emotions as energy—energy that can propel us forward instead of holding us back?

For example, imagine Lily, a student working on a challenging puzzle. When she faces a roadblock and becomes frustrated, she doesn't let it defeat her. Instead, she recognizes that frustration as a signal: "Something's not working. I need a new approach." This shift in mindset turns her frustration into motivation. It drives her to persist, seek help, or take a short break to reframe her thinking. That emotional energy—the frustration—isn't wasted; it becomes the fuel for her resilience.

This shift in perspective is the core of emotional intelligence: understanding that emotions, even the difficult ones, are not inherently negative. When channeled effectively, they can drive us to try harder, think creatively, and approach problems from new angles.

Activity: The "Feel and Fuel" Game

This fun and interactive activity helps students reframe their emotions as sources of energy that can drive them toward positive action.

1. **Name That Feeling**: Start by having students share how they're feeling. It could be anything from happy, frustrated, excited, or nervous.
2. **Fuel Up**: Ask students to brainstorm ways each feeling can be used as energy. For example, frustration can push us to find a new solution, while excitement can fuel creativity. By doing this, students learn that emotions are not just reactions; they can be catalysts for positive action.
3. **Action Stations**: Set up different stations where students can role-play or demonstrate how to manage emotions in various situations. One station could focus on asking for help when feeling frustrated, another on taking a break when feeling overwhelmed, and another on celebrating small successes when feeling accomplished.
4. **Celebrate Wins**: Finish the activity by celebrating every student who shares their emotional insights or demonstrates new emotional regulation strategies. Recognize the importance of emotional awareness and growth in the classroom.

This activity not only helps students see the value of their emotions but also gives them tools to transform them into positive actions, reinforcing the idea that emotions can be powerful motivators for success.

The Art of Emotional Self-Regulation: Mastering the "Pause, Breathe, Respond" Trick

Self-regulation is like having a remote control for your emotions, enabling you to slow down and steer in a better direction when emotions run high. This skill helps students manage stress, anxiety, and other strong emotions, especially in situations that might otherwise lead to impulsive behavior.

Max, a student who is nervous about an upcoming test, uses the "Pause, Breathe, Respond" method:

1. **Pause**: Before reacting impulsively, Max takes a moment to stop and reflect on his emotions. This brief pause creates space between the feeling and the response.
2. **Breathe**: Max takes deep, slow breaths to calm himself and regulate his physiological response to stress. Breathing helps reset the body's stress response, promoting a sense of calm and control.
3. **Respond**: Max then asks himself, "What's the best way to handle this test?" This reflective question encourages him to make a rational, thoughtful decision instead of reacting emotionally. It helps him focus on the actions he can take, such as reviewing his notes, practicing relaxation techniques, or asking for clarification.

Building an Emotional Resilience Toolbox

Emotional resilience doesn't come naturally to everyone, but it can be developed with practice. Here are a few strategies to help students build their resilience toolbox:

- **Positive Affirmations**: Encourage students to repeat empowering phrases, such as, "I can handle this," when facing tough situations. This helps them build self-confidence and stay optimistic in the face of adversity.
- **Mindfulness**: Introduce short mindfulness exercises, such as focusing on the breath or guided visualization, to help students stay present and grounded. These techniques can be particularly helpful when students are feeling overwhelmed or distracted.
- **Growth Mindset**: Teach students that mistakes are not failures but opportunities for growth. When they understand that intelligence and abilities can be developed through effort and persistence, they become more resilient in the face of challenges.

These strategies, when practiced regularly, can help students develop the emotional resilience needed to overcome setbacks and thrive both academically and personally.

Final Thoughts: The Importance of Emotional Intelligence

Emotional intelligence isn't just about feeling good—it's about feeling what's real and then using that awareness to navigate life effectively. When we teach students to understand, manage, and use their emotions as tools, we empower them to face whatever comes their way with confidence, resilience, and strength. Emotional intelligence is not just a skill for school—it's a life skill. And the best part? It can be developed, nurtured, and celebrated every day in our classrooms.

6
Encouraging Students to Learn from Failure

When I was a teacher, my life science class was one of my favorite subjects to teach. Science is all about discovery, experimentation, and, most importantly, failure. I made it a point to design lessons that required my students to test ideas, observe outcomes, and adjust their thinking. But despite my best efforts to create a classroom culture that welcomed mistakes, many of my students still feared failure.

One year, I had a student named Josh who was particularly bright but also a perfectionist. We were working on an experiment to test the effects of different variables on plant growth. The goal was for students to make predictions, test their hypotheses, and analyze what worked and what didn't. Josh carefully designed his experiment, measuring soil pH, tracking sunlight exposure, and meticulously recording data. But when his plants started wilting instead of thriving, he was devastated.

"I did everything right," he said, frustration in his voice. "Why isn't it working?"

I smiled. "Josh, let me ask you something. What do scientists do when an experiment doesn't go as planned?"

He hesitated. "They... try again?"

"Exactly. Failure isn't the opposite of success—it's part of it. What can you learn from this?"

That moment was a turning point for Josh, and for many of my students who realized that setbacks weren't dead ends, but learning opportunities. And as I look back at my years in education, I realize that some of the strongest students weren't the ones who always succeeded, but the ones who learned how to handle failure and push forward.

Why Failure Matters

In education, we often focus on academic excellence, but what about the emotional strength and determination needed to push through challenges? The students who grow up to be the strongest—emotionally and mentally—aren't necessarily the ones who succeed on the first try. They are the ones who learn how to face failure, pick themselves back up, and try again.

Resilience—the ability to bounce back from setbacks—isn't something that just happens; it's cultivated through persistence, grit, and perseverance. Just as muscles grow stronger when we push them to their limits, resilience strengthens when students are challenged, fail, and try again.

This chapter is all about helping students see failure not as a dead-end, but as a stepping stone to growth. We'll explore how to create a classroom environment that normalizes mistakes, encourages persistence, and equips students with the mindset needed to embrace challenges rather than fear them.

The Role of Failure in Building Resilience

Failure. It's a word that strikes fear into the hearts of many—both students and teachers alike. But what if we told you that failure isn't something to avoid, but something to embrace? That it is, in fact, one of the most powerful tools for building resilience?

Many students fear failure because they associate it with inadequacy. They may believe that failing means they're not good enough or that they should just give up. However, with a simple shift in perspective, failure can transform from a source of fear into a powerful learning opportunity.

In the context of science and many other subjects, failure teaches valuable lessons. When students experiment, they learn not only about the subject but about themselves. They learn about their strengths, their weaknesses, their ability to adapt, and their problem-solving skills. Failure, then, is a classroom teacher in its own right, revealing to students the importance of not just finding answers, but of navigating the unknown.

Failing Forward

One of the most empowering ways to approach failure is to fail forward—a concept that encourages students to view failure not as a setback but as a step toward growth and learning.

Think of Thomas Edison, who famously said, "I have not failed. I've just found 10,000 ways that won't work." Or Michael Jordan, who was cut from his high school basketball team but went on to become one of the greatest athletes in history. These stories remind us that success is often built on the lessons learned from failure.

As a teacher, you can encourage this mindset by framing mistakes as a natural part of the learning process. Instead of penalizing students for errors, celebrate the opportunity to improve. Try saying, "Mistakes are proof that we are trying," or "Every time we fail, we get one step closer to success."

Another crucial aspect of failing forward is **sticktoitiveness**— the ability to keep going despite setbacks. Just as scientists expect their experiments to fail and keep refining their approaches, students should learn to persist and keep trying. The key to long-term success often isn't avoiding failure; it's having the perseverance to push through it.

When students understand that failure is just a stepping stone, they develop the inner fortitude to tackle bigger challenges. Sticktoitiveness is about resilience in action, and it's a skill that can serve students far beyond the classroom.

The Disney Story: Perseverance Through Rejection

One of the most well-known stories of perseverance comes from Walt Disney, who faced rejection after rejection before achieving success.

Before he created the Magic Kingdom we all recognize, Disney was fired from a newspaper job for "lack of imagination" and "no good ideas." He pitched the idea of a theme park to investors who dismissed it as unrealistic. Again and again, he heard "no."

But Disney didn't let failure stop him. Instead of giving up, he pushed forward, refining his ideas and learning from each rejection. Eventually, his persistence led to the creation of Disneyland, and later, an entire media empire that still inspires millions today.

The Disney story exemplifies sticktoitiveness. It's not just about having an idea or a goal; it's about the grit to keep going even when others say no. And that's the kind of mindset that transforms failure into success.

The Disney Lesson for Your Classroom

What if we taught our students that rejection is not the end? What if we showed them that failure isn't something to fear, but something that can eventually lead to greatness?

When students struggle—whether it's a difficult math problem, a tricky science experiment, or a new skill—they need to see obstacles as opportunities. Encouraging them to "fail forward" can help them develop the resilience to persist, no matter the challenge.

If they can approach failure the way Disney approached rejection, they'll see that the journey to success is full of bumps, twists, and detours—but it's these very detours that lead to growth. Their ability to maintain sticktoitiveness in the face of challenges will ultimately determine their ability to achieve their goals.

Creating a "Fail-Safe" Classroom Environment

To truly help students build resilience, you must create a fail-safe environment—one where students feel safe taking risks without the fear of judgment.

In such an environment, students aren't afraid to speak up, make mistakes, and try new things. They're empowered to explore, experiment, and fail—knowing that these failures are simply part of the process.

A fail-safe classroom should focus on effort, not just results. Celebrate each step along the way, not just the final product. And when students do make mistakes, approach them with compassion and a mindset that values growth.

Strategies for Building a Resilient Classroom Culture

1. **Normalize Mistakes** – Encourage students to see mistakes as part of the learning process. Share personal stories of times you failed and how those moments ultimately helped you grow.
2. **Reward the Process, Not Just the Result** – Praise the effort students put into their work, not just the final outcome.
3. **Promote a Growth Mindset** – Teach students that their abilities aren't fixed. They can grow and improve with effort, making challenges and opportunities for development.
4. **Develop Sticktoitiveness** – Teach your students the importance of perseverance. Let them know that sticking with a problem or challenge, even when it seems impossible, is a skill that will serve them well for the rest of their lives.

Resilience in the Face of Trauma

Not all students experience failure in the same way. Some face significant trauma—whether it's the loss of a parent, abuse, or living in high-stress environments. For these students, resilience-building strategies must be approached with care.

Trauma-Informed Resilience

Trauma affects a child's brain development and emotional regulation, making it difficult to cope with stress. As educators, it's essential to recognize that trauma impacts not just behavior, but also how a child processes the world around them.
To support these students:

- ♦ Provide a sense of safety and stability. Establish predictable routines and consistent support.
- ♦ Build trust through relationships. Be the teacher who shows up every day with empathy, compassion, and reliability.
- ♦ Teach self-regulation skills. Incorporate mindfulness and breathing exercises into daily routines to help students manage their emotions.

The Power of Praising Effort Over Results

Society tends to emphasize outcomes—perfect test scores, trophies, straight A's. But when it comes to resilience, the real key is effort.

When we focus too much on results, we create an environment where success is measured by a fixed standard. This can be discouraging for students who are still developing their skills. But when we praise effort, we reinforce the idea that persistence and hard work lead to growth.

How to Praise Effort in the Classroom

1. **Focus on the Process** – Instead of saying, "You got an A! Great job!" try, "I can see you worked really hard on this project. Your effort really paid off!"

2. **Encourage Persistence** – When a student struggles, remind them that perseverance is key.
3. **Praise Strategies, Not Just Results** – Acknowledge the problem-solving process, not just the final answer.
4. **Promote a Growth Mindset** – Reinforce the idea that learning is a journey, and effort is what leads to progress.

Strategies for Building Resilience in the Classroom

To help students embrace failure as part of their growth, we can integrate hands-on activities and reflective practices into the classroom. Below are some strategies that create opportunities for students to develop resilience and a growth mindset.

Growth Mindset Journals

Have students keep journals where they reflect on their experiences with failure. In each entry, students should describe a challenge they faced, how they handled it, and what they could do differently next time. This activity encourages students to reframe failures, turning them into opportunities for growth. By consistently reflecting on how they approach challenges, students can internalize the belief that their abilities can improve with effort and perseverance.

"Fail Forward" Success Stories

Share inspiring stories of famous figures who failed before achieving success, such as Thomas Edison's many attempts before inventing the light bulb, or Michael Jordan's early career setbacks. After sharing these stories, have students create their own "Fail Forward" stories. Students can write or present their own personal experiences of failure and how they overcame them. This exercise promotes self-reflection and shows students that even highly successful people face and learn from failure.

Team Problem-Solving Challenges

Design a classroom challenge where students must work in groups to solve a problem. However, the challenge is meant to be difficult, and students are expected to fail at first. The goal is to foster collaboration and resilience as students work together, fail together, and ultimately learn from their experiences. After the challenge, facilitate a group discussion on what strategies worked, what didn't, and how they can improve their problem-solving approach next time. This exercise reinforces the idea that failure is a collective experience and can lead to better teamwork and improved outcomes.

Resilience Through Art
Let students express their feelings about failure through art. Whether it's drawing, painting, or creating a visual representation of their experiences, this activity provides a creative outlet for students to process and reflect on failure in a personal way. For students who struggle to articulate their emotions verbally, art becomes an alternative way to express their challenges and growth. This activity not only helps students process failure but also gives them a tangible representation of their resilience.

These activities are designed to create a classroom culture where failure is normalized, and resilience is celebrated. When students can reflect on their failures and see them as learning opportunities, they develop the skills to persevere through challenges. By integrating these strategies into the classroom, we provide students with the tools they need to navigate failure with confidence and embrace the journey of growth.

Final Thoughts: Resilience Starts with Learning to Fail

By encouraging persistence, embracing failure, and praising effort, we're not just helping students succeed academically—we're helping them develop the emotional strength to face life's challenges.

Teaching resilience isn't about making things easier. It's about giving students the confidence to struggle, fail, and try again. When they realize that failure isn't an endpoint but a beginning, they'll carry that lesson far beyond the classroom.

Because tough times don't last—but students who learn to fail, adapt, and persevere do.

7

Building Autonomy and Self-Regulation

As educators, we often hear about the importance of resilience—the ability to bounce back from adversity, maintain focus despite challenges, and continue striving toward goals even when faced with setbacks. In Chapter 5, we explored the foundational skill of self-regulation as a key factor in resilience. In this chapter, we'll dive deeper, examining how self-regulation not only supports academic achievement but also fosters autonomy and emotional intelligence, two critical components for long-term success.

Self-regulation isn't just about discipline; it's about empowering students to manage their emotions, behaviors, and thoughts. When students can self-regulate, they are better equipped to handle challenges, focus in the classroom, and stay engaged in their learning. It's a skill that supports their overall well-being and, in turn, fosters resilience.

Throughout my career, I've come to realize that fostering self-regulation is one of the most impactful things we can do as teachers. In this chapter, we will explore how to build self-regulation skills in your classroom and why it's crucial for helping students develop resilience in both their academic and personal lives.

The Power of Self-Regulation in Learning

One of the most important lessons I learned early in my teaching career was that self-regulation isn't just about discipline—it's about empowerment. I vividly remember one student, let's call him Alex. Alex was a bright and capable student, but he had a difficult time staying seated for long periods of time. His energy seemed boundless, and I often found him squirming in his chair, fidgeting with his pencil, or distracted by the smallest sounds in the classroom. The conventional wisdom at the time told me that I should enforce stricter rules—perhaps have him sit still in his seat until he could learn to focus.

But after some reflection, I realized this approach might not be the best for him. Instead of forcing Alex to conform to the traditional classroom structure, I decided to try something different: I gave him the opportunity to move. I allowed him to go to the back of the room and do sit-ups and push-ups when he needed a break. The first few times, it was a little disruptive, and I could see other students looking over at him, wondering what was happening. Some of them even asked, "Why can he get up and move around when we have to stay in our seats?"

But after a few days, something remarkable happened: Alex's focus improved dramatically. His anxiety about staying still melted away, and he began to engage more deeply in the lessons. Instead of struggling to remain seated, he was now able to regulate his own energy productively. His performance soared, and more importantly, he began to feel in control of his learning experience.

This experience taught me something important: self-regulation is not about controlling students; it's about giving them the tools to manage their own energy, emotions, and attention. When students have the freedom to regulate themselves, they can thrive in ways that rigid, one-size-fits-all approaches never would allow.

Understanding Self-Regulation

Self-regulation is a crucial skill that enables students to manage their emotions, behaviors, and thoughts in ways that promote learning and overall well-being. It's what helps students stay focused despite distractions, persist through challenges, and adapt to new situations. When students develop self-regulation, they are better equipped to handle the ups and downs of both academic and social life, which are essential components of resilience.

Research has shown that self-regulation is one of the most reliable predictors of academic success, even more so than IQ. A study from the University of Minnesota found that children who could regulate their emotions and behaviors at an early age performed better academically throughout their schooling (source: University of Minnesota, "Emotional Self-Regulation and Academic Performance in Children," Journal of Early Childhood Education, 2014). These students were more likely to maintain focus in the classroom, solve problems effectively, and make decisions that supported their long-term goals.

However, self-regulation isn't just beneficial for academic achievement. It also plays a pivotal role in mental and emotional health. Students who regulate their emotions effectively tend to have stronger relationships with their peers and teachers, are less likely to experience anxiety, and possess better coping mechanisms when faced with difficult situations.

Activity for Self-Regulation

Goal-Setting Reflection
Encourage students to set one academic or personal goal they wish to achieve over the next month. Have them break that goal down into smaller, actionable steps. Then, provide time for them to reflect on the actions they can take daily to make progress toward their goal, using strategies like prioritizing tasks, breaking them into smaller pieces, and taking regular breaks to avoid overwhelm.

Creating a Classroom That Supports Self-Regulation

As educators, we can foster self-regulation in our students by creating a classroom environment that supports movement, reflection, and autonomy. Instead of enforcing rigid discipline or expecting students to sit still and focus for hours on end, we can provide opportunities for them to regulate themselves in healthy, constructive ways.

Here are some strategies that have proven effective in promoting self-regulation in the classroom:

Flexible Seating and Movement Breaks

Students who struggle with focus often benefit from flexible seating arrangements and the option to move. Rigid seating assignments can make it difficult for some students to concentrate, especially those who have excess energy or need to move in order to focus. Allowing students to choose where they sit, or even to stand at a standing desk or use a balance ball, can help them regulate their attention and energy levels.

Additionally, short, structured movement breaks throughout the day can help prevent frustration and increase engagement. For example, after 20 minutes of focused work, allow students to take a quick break to stretch, walk around the room, or do a brief physical activity like jumping jacks or stretching. This helps reset their brains and bodies, preparing them to refocus on the next task.

Mindful Transitions

Transitions between activities can often be a chaotic time in the classroom. Instead of abrupt shifts that leave students feeling flustered, take a few minutes to guide them through a mindful transition. Techniques such as deep breathing, stretching, or a brief reflection period can help students reset and refocus. Encourage students to pause, take a deep breath, and think about what they need to do next. This not only helps with self-regulation but also fosters mindfulness—a skill that can help students manage stress and remain calm in challenging situations.

Personalized Coping Strategies

Every student is different, and so are their needs when it comes to self-regulation. Some students may need sensory tools, such as fidget spinners or noise-canceling headphones, while others might benefit from calming music or a quiet space to regroup. By offering a variety of strategies, teachers can help students find what works best for them.

For example, if a student becomes easily overwhelmed by loud noises, offering them noise-canceling headphones during group work or testing can help them focus. Alternatively, a student who struggles with fidgeting may benefit from using a stress ball or other tactile tools to help them stay engaged without distracting others.

Teaching Students to Recognize Their Own Needs

Self-regulation isn't just about external strategies—it's also about helping students develop internal awareness. We want students to recognize when they are becoming overwhelmed and need a break, rather than pushing through frustration until they shut down. Teaching students to identify their emotional states and take action to regulate their feelings is an essential part of building resilience.

For example, I had a student named Jack who would completely shut down whenever he became frustrated. Instead of forcing him to continue working through his frustration, I worked with him to develop a signal—a simple hand gesture—that he could use when he needed a break. This small adjustment allowed Jack to communicate his needs without disrupting the class, and it transformed his ability to engage in learning.

Helping students recognize when they need a break or a moment of self-regulation can prevent emotional overload and build their confidence in managing their emotions.

The Role of Emotional Regulation

Emotions are deeply intertwined with self-regulation. When students experience emotions like frustration, anxiety, or boredom, their ability to focus, learn, and engage can be significantly impacted. Intense emotions often trigger physiological responses like increased heart rate, shallow breathing, or the feeling of being overwhelmed. These responses can make it difficult for students to process information, stay on task, and participate in learning.

As educators, we play a key role in helping students navigate these emotional challenges. By recognizing the emotional components of self-regulation, we can implement strategies that allow students to manage their feelings, regain focus, and engage effectively in their studies. This improves not only their emotional intelligence but also enhances their overall learning process.

Activity for Emotional Regulation: Emotion Check-In

At the start of each class, have students briefly assess how they are feeling on a scale from 1 to 5, with 1 being a negative emotion (like frustration or anxiety) and 5 being calm and focused. This helps students identify their emotional state and reflect on the strategies they might need to self-regulate (such as deep breathing, moving around, or taking a moment to pause). This simple check-in promotes self-awareness and provides an opportunity for students to communicate their needs in a non-disruptive way (Huebner, Suldo, & Valois, 2004).

Deep Breathing for Emotional Regulation

One powerful tool for emotional regulation is deep breathing. When students are overwhelmed or anxious, deep breathing helps calm their nervous systems and focus their attention. This strategy can be incorporated into classroom routines and used as a go-to tool for students to regain composure. Research shows that deep breathing activates the parasympathetic nervous system, reducing stress and improving emotional regulation (Zaccaro, O'Driscoll, & Salas, 2018; Sze & Herring, 2017).

Activity for Emotional Regulation: Mindful Breathing

Guide students through a deep-breathing exercise by asking them to close their eyes, take three slow, deep breaths, and focus on the sensation of their breath entering and leaving their bodies. This simple exercise helps reset their emotional state and prepares them to re-engage in the lesson. Studies have shown that mindful breathing helps to reduce stress and improve focus and emotional regulation, making it an effective tool for students (Zeidan, Johnson, Diamond, & David, 2010).

Space for Self-Regulation

Providing students with a designated space to self-regulate can be an effective strategy for supporting emotional regulation. This space could include options for physical activities like push-ups, or relaxation strategies like deep breathing. Research indicates that allowing children to engage in physical activity or relaxation in designated areas can improve emotional well-being and academic engagement (Burdette & Whitaker, 2005; Sari & Tabak, 2017).

Incorporating emotional regulation strategies such as emotion check-ins, deep breathing exercises, and designated self-regulation spaces can significantly enhance students' ability to manage their emotions and focus in the classroom. By encouraging students to assess their emotional states and implement calming techniques like deep breathing or physical activity, educators can foster a supportive environment that promotes self-awareness and emotional well-being. Research underscores the effectiveness of these strategies in reducing stress, improving focus, and ultimately enhancing academic engagement. These practices not only help students regain composure but also empower them with the tools to navigate emotional challenges both in and outside the classroom.

Validating Emotions

One of the first steps in addressing emotional regulation is validating students' emotions. Validating doesn't mean agreeing with the emotion but rather recognizing and acknowledging that the student's feelings are real and worthy of attention. When we validate emotions, we send a message that it's okay to feel frustrated, anxious, or upset—it's part of being human. This helps to normalize their experiences and reduces the likelihood of students suppressing their feelings, which can lead to further stress or anxiety.

For example, when a student expresses frustration over a math problem, saying, "Don't worry about it," can invalidate their feelings, suggesting that their frustration is unimportant. Instead, try saying something like, "I can see this is really challenging for you. It's okay to feel frustrated, and we'll work through it together." This approach acknowledges the emotion and opens up a space for collaboration, easing the tension and fostering a positive learning environment.

Activity Ideas for Validating Emotions:

- **Emotion Check-In:** Have students use a simple tool like a feelings chart or emoji scale to check in with their emotions at the start of each day or before a lesson. This allows them to identify and express how they're feeling, helping you understand their emotional state.
- **Feelings Journal:** Encourage students to keep a journal where they write down or draw about their emotions and experiences during the school day. This can be especially useful for students who struggle with verbal expression. Later, they can reflect on how they managed their emotions during various activities.
- **Group Reflection:** After a challenging activity or task, hold a brief group discussion where students can share how they felt and how they overcame challenges. This promotes emotional validation and encourages others to recognize that it's okay to struggle and seek support.

Modeling Self-Regulation

Students often learn more from our actions than our words, so modeling self-regulation is a powerful teaching strategy. When we, as educators, demonstrate how to cope with difficult emotions—through calm responses to challenges, using positive self-talk, or openly expressing how we handle stress—we teach students the value of self-regulation through observation.

For example, if you encounter a stressful situation, verbalizing your thought process can provide valuable learning moments. Saying something like, "I'm feeling a little frustrated right now, but I know I can take a deep breath and break this problem down into smaller steps," not only models how to regulate emotions but also shows students that it's okay to experience negative emotions as long as we learn to manage them effectively.
Activity Ideas for Modeling Self-Regulation:

- **Think-Alouds:** During difficult tasks, use "think-alouds" where you verbally walk students through your thought process. For example, when approaching a challenging math problem or a classroom disruption, say things like, "I'm feeling stressed, but I'm going to take a moment to breathe and refocus." This shows them how to approach difficult moments with a calm mindset.
- **Mindfulness Moments:** Incorporate short mindfulness activities into the day. These could be as simple as guiding students through a 1-minute breathing exercise before a test or during transitions. This allows students to see you practicing self-regulation in real time.
- **Stress-Busting Techniques:** Share your personal strategies for managing stress, such as taking deep breaths, stretching, or pausing to reflect. Encourage students to develop their own techniques and make them part of classroom routines.

The Power of Choice and Autonomy

One of the most effective ways to support self-regulation is by giving students a sense of control over their learning. Autonomy fosters intrinsic motivation, increases engagement, and encourages responsibility. When students feel like they have a voice in their education, they're more likely to take ownership of their behavior and the outcomes of their work.

Simple acts of allowing students to make choices can significantly enhance their ability to self-regulate. When students choose how to approach a task or organize their work, they are more invested in the process. They also develop skills in managing their time, emotions, and energy in ways that support their academic success.

Activity Ideas for Promoting Autonomy and Choice:
- **Choice Boards:** Create a "choice board" with different types of activities or assignments. For example, students could choose whether they want to demonstrate mastery of a concept through a written report, an oral presentation, or a creative project. This allows students to take ownership of how they demonstrate what they've learned.
- **Flexible Seating:** Allow students to choose where they sit during independent work or group activities. Some may prefer a quiet corner, while others may thrive in a group setting. This freedom of choice can help students feel more comfortable and in control of their learning environment.
- **Self-Directed Learning Projects:** Provide opportunities for students to explore topics of their own interest. Give them the autonomy to select a subject, research it, and present their findings in a format that suits their style—whether through a digital project, a visual presentation, or a traditional essay.
- **Time Management:** Teach students how to manage their own learning time. For example, provide them with a set of tasks for the day and let them decide the order in which they complete them, helping them prioritize and regulate their time effectively.

By giving students these opportunities for choice and autonomy, we're not just fostering self-regulation; we're teaching them how to make thoughtful decisions, how to be responsible for their learning, and how to manage their actions in a way that leads to success.

Final Thoughts: Empowering Students Through Self-Regulation

Self-regulation is one of the most powerful skills we can teach our students, and its impact goes far beyond just classroom behavior. It equips students with the tools they need to navigate life's challenges with confidence, resilience, and success. In our classrooms, when we foster self-regulation, we are not only helping students perform better academically, but we are setting them up for success in all areas of life.

By encouraging movement, emotional awareness, autonomy, and personalized strategies, we create a learning environment that goes beyond traditional teaching methods. It becomes one where students thrive, gaining the ability to manage their own behavior and emotions effectively. They learn how to focus, how to stay calm under pressure, and how to rebound from setbacks. These are not just academic skills—they are life skills that they will carry with them into adulthood.

Empowering students to regulate themselves is also a powerful tool for building resilience. Resilience is the foundation that helps them persist through difficulties, manage stress, and find solutions to problems—whether in the classroom or beyond. When we teach self-regulation, we are investing in their future success, helping them to develop the inner strength they need to face whatever life may bring. This is a skill that pays dividends over time, fostering not only academic success but emotional well-being as well.

It's equally important to model and validate emotional regulation. When we acknowledge students' emotions and help them manage their feelings, we teach them valuable coping strategies. This modeling creates an environment where students feel supported, understood, and empowered to handle their emotions in a healthy way. Acknowledging their feelings not only helps students build emotional resilience but also enhances their academic achievement. They become more engaged, more motivated, and more confident in their ability to tackle challenges head-on.

By providing students with opportunities to move, reflect, and make decisions about their learning, we allow them to take ownership of their behavior and outcomes. Movement breaks, mindful transitions, and personalized coping strategies are all essential components in helping students regulate their energy and emotions. These strategies give students the power to control their focus and stay engaged in their learning, building their capacity for self-regulation and self-control.

As we continue to teach, nurture, and support self-regulation in our students, we equip them with the lifelong skills they need for success—not only in school but in every aspect of their lives. This focus on self-regulation is an investment in their future, one that will pay off in their academic journey and beyond. It's a powerful, ongoing process of building resilience, developing emotional intelligence, and creating the foundation for lifelong success.

8
Harnessing the Power of Play and Physical Activity

Welcome to Chapter 8, where we're trading in our textbooks for a playground mindset! In this chapter, we're going to explore how play and physical activity aren't just fun ways to pass the time—they're powerful tools for building resilience in our young learners. We'll dive into the science and heart of play, share inspiring stories (including some amazing examples from the animal kingdom), and offer a wealth of practical, classroom-friendly strategies for K–5 teachers. So, lace up your sneakers, stretch those imaginations, and get ready to discover how movement and play can unlock a world of emotional strength, creative problem-solving, and resilience.

A Wild Introduction: Lessons from Nature's Playful Pioneers

Before we jump into the nitty-gritty of playful resilience, let's take a moment to look at nature for inspiration. Have you ever watched a litter of lion cubs at play? These little bundles of fur are a masterclass in resilience-building. Lion cubs spend countless hours tumbling, pouncing, and chasing one another—not just for fun, but to develop the skills they need to survive in the wild.

Through their playful antics, they learn coordination, strength, social skills, and even how to handle setbacks gracefully when their game doesn't go as planned.

This isn't unique to lion cubs; it's a phenomenon seen in nearly all mammals. From puppies learning to navigate their environment to chimpanzees engaging in playful wrestling, play is a universal language of growth and adaptation. These young animals are not simply "wasting time" when they play; they are actively rewiring their brains, developing critical survival skills, and learning how to bounce back from challenges—all in a low-risk, joyful environment (Pellis & Pellis, 2009).

For our young learners, play works in much the same way. When children engage in play and physical activity, they practice problem-solving, emotional regulation, and teamwork. They learn that mistakes are part of the process and that every tumble or misstep is just a stepping stone to greater strength. In our classrooms, we have the opportunity to harness this natural energy and channel it into building resilience that lasts a lifetime.

The Incredible Role of Play and Physical Activity in Building Resilience

Play as a Tool for Resilience

Play is much more than a way for children to have fun—it's a vital tool for building resilience. Research shows that when children engage in play, they develop the skills to manage stress and navigate adversity. Think of play as a rehearsal for life. It gives children the freedom to experiment, take risks, and learn from their mistakes without real-world consequences. Here's how play nurtures resilience:

- ♦ **Experimentation and Risk-Taking**: During play, children try out new ideas. For instance, building a block tower that eventually tumbles teaches them that failure is temporary and that they can try again. It's a hands-on lesson in persistence and creativity (Ginsburg, 2007).

- **Problem-Solving**: Every game presents mini-challenges. Whether it's figuring out the best strategy in a game of tag or solving a puzzle during a play-based math activity, children are constantly learning to think on their feet and adjust their approach (Bodrova & Leong, 2007).
- **Emotional Regulation**: Play naturally exposes children to a range of emotions. They experience the joy of success and the frustration of setbacks. Over time, this helps them learn to manage their feelings, recover from disappointments, and even celebrate their progress (Greenberg et al., 2003).
- **Social Skills and Empathy**: When children play together, they negotiate roles, share resources, and resolve conflicts. These interactions build essential social skills, teaching them the importance of empathy, cooperation, and communication—key components of resilience (Bodrova & Leong, 2007).

Physical Activity and Mental Strength

Just as exercise strengthens the body, physical activity is a powerful booster for mental toughness. Here's how movement contributes to building resilience:

- **Stress Reduction**: When children engage in physical activity, their bodies release endorphins—the "feel-good" hormones. These hormones help reduce anxiety and create a sense of calm, allowing children to manage stress more effectively (Singh et al., 2008).
- **Mood Enhancement**: Physical activity has an immediate impact on mood. A burst of energy on the playground or a quick game of tag can lift spirits and help children face challenges with a positive outlook (Salmon, 2001).
- **Persistence and Perseverance**: Tackling a physical challenge—like climbing a jungle gym or mastering a new dance move—teaches children that perseverance pays off. They learn that effort and practice can lead to improvement, building confidence that spills over into other areas of life (Murray & Ramstetter, 2013).

- **Cognitive Benefits**: Studies have shown that physical activity increases blood flow to the brain, enhancing concentration, memory, and overall cognitive function. A well-oxygenated brain is more adept at problem-solving and adapting to new challenges, further strengthening resilience (Hillman et al., 2008).

The Role of Team Sports and Group Play

Group activities and team sports offer a special kind of resilience training. They teach children that no one has to face challenges alone. Here's what they gain from group play:

- **Collaboration and Teamwork**: In team sports, every player has a role. Children learn that working together, sharing ideas, and supporting one another can lead to success—even if it's not about winning the game (Ewing et al., 2002).
- **Empathy and Communication**: Group play requires children to listen, share, and sometimes compromise. These interactions nurture empathy and help them understand different perspectives, essential skills for both academic and personal success (Ewing et al., 2002).
- **Handling Setbacks Together**: In any team activity, setbacks are inevitable. Whether it's a lost game or a failed group challenge, children learn to view these setbacks as collective learning opportunities (Snyder et al., 2015).
- **Building a Sense of Belonging**: Being part of a team or group activity fosters a strong sense of community and belonging. This connection reinforces the idea that challenges are easier to overcome when you have a supportive network around you (Snyder et al., 2015).

Action Steps for Educators: Bringing Playful Resilience to Life

Now that we understand the powerful role of play and physical activity in building resilience, let's dive into practical strategies that you, as a K–5 educator, can implement in your classroom. These actionable steps will help you create an environment where every child can flourish through movement, play, and positive social interaction.

1. Incorporate Movement into the Classroom

Even in the midst of academic lessons, integrating movement can transform the learning environment. Here are some ideas:

- **Brain Breaks:**
  Every 20–30 minutes, lead your class in a short, energizing activity. This could be a quick game of "Simon Says," a mini dance party, or a simple stretch routine. These breaks help reset students' focus and release pent-up energy.
- **Transition Activities:**
  Use movement to signal transitions between subjects. For example, when moving from a quiet reading session to a more active lesson, have the class stand up and perform a series of fun stretches or a quick "follow the leader" game.
- **Active Learning Stations:**
  Create learning stations that incorporate movement. A reading station might involve a short walk to a "story corner" set up in a different area of the classroom. A math station could include a puzzle that requires physical manipulation of objects.
- **Outdoor Lessons:**
  Whenever possible, take your lessons outside. Fresh air and natural light can boost students' mood and engagement. Consider outdoor math scavenger hunts, nature walks to discuss science topics, or story circles in a nearby park.

2. Embrace Play-Based Learning

Transform your curriculum by integrating play into academic learning. Play-based learning not only makes lessons more engaging but also builds resilience through experimentation and creativity.

- **Interactive Games:**
  Design games that tie into your lesson objectives. For instance, a spelling game where students hop on numbered spots for each letter or a math game that uses movement to represent different operations can make learning fun and dynamic.
- **Role-Playing Scenarios:**
  Create scenarios that allow students to act out real-life situations. For example, set up a "store" where students practice math skills while role-playing as customers and cashiers. This not only reinforces academic content but also builds communication and problem-solving skills.
- **Game-Based Challenges:**
  Introduce challenges that blend cognitive and physical efforts. A "math relay" where each correct answer lets the team move closer to the finish line or a science scavenger hunt that requires both investigation and teamwork can make academic content more interactive.
- **Imaginative Play:**
  Allocate time for unstructured play where students are free to explore their imaginations. Encourage activities such as building forts, creating imaginative stories, or designing their own games. This free play is essential for creativity and resilience.

3. Organize Sports and Group Challenges

Team sports and group challenges are invaluable for developing social skills, empathy, and collective resilience. Here are some ideas to bring more group activity into your classroom:

- **Team Sports:**
  Organize simple team sports like kickball, soccer, or capture the flag during recess or physical education classes. Emphasize fun and participation over competition. Discuss with your class how every effort counts and how working together makes challenges easier.
- **Cooperative Games:**
  Introduce cooperative games that require collaboration. A game like "Human Knot," where students work

together to untangle themselves without letting go of each other's hands, builds trust, communication, and creative problem-solving.
- **Group Challenges:**
  Create challenges that require the entire class to work as a team. For instance, set up a building challenge where groups use recycled materials to construct the tallest tower or design an obstacle course where each student's participation is essential for the team to succeed.
- **Reflection Sessions:**
  After group activities, hold a brief reflection session. Ask questions like, "What did we learn about teamwork today?" or "How did we overcome our challenges together?" This helps reinforce the lessons of resilience and collective support.

Integrating Playful Resilience into Daily Routines

Incorporating the power of play into your classroom isn't a one-time event—it's a continuous journey. Here are some strategies to make playful resilience a natural part of your daily routines:

Make It a Daily Habit

- **Morning Energizers:**
  Start each day with a fun, active routine. Whether it's a quick dance session, a "follow the leader" game, or a series of stretching exercises, these activities set a positive tone for the day.
- **Learning Through Play:**
  Weave play-based activities into your lesson plans. Even in subjects like math or reading, interactive games, and playful challenges can make the content more engaging and relatable.
- **Mindful Movement:**
  Combine movement with mindfulness. For example, after a high-energy game, guide your students through

a calming, slow-paced activity where they focus on deep breathing and reflect on how the activity made them feel.

Involve Everyone
- **Inclusive Games:**
Design games and activities that are accessible to every student. Adapt rules or roles as needed so that each child, regardless of physical ability or skill level, can participate and contribute.
- **Peer Leadership:**
Encourage older or more confident students to lead activities or mentor their peers. This not only reinforces their own skills but also helps build a supportive classroom community.
- **Family Engagement:**
Share your playful resilience strategies with families. Send home newsletters or organize school events where parents can see firsthand how play is being used to build resilience. When families understand these methods, they can reinforce them at home.

Reflect and Celebrate
- **Regular Reflection:**
Build time into your schedule for students to reflect on their play experiences. Ask them to share what challenges they faced during a game and what they learned from overcoming those challenges. This reflection helps solidify the connection between play, learning, and resilience.
- **Celebrate Effort:**
Create a classroom culture where every effort is recognized and celebrated. Whether it's through a "Resilience Star" chart, stickers, or shout-outs during class, make sure that every small victory is acknowledged.
- **Visual Reminders:**
Decorate your classroom with posters, charts, or even student-created art that highlights the benefits of play and movement. Visual cues can serve as daily reminders of the importance of resilience and teamwork.

Stories of Playful Resilience in Action

To truly appreciate the impact of play and physical activity on resilience, let's look at some inspiring stories from classrooms—and even from nature—that show how playful experiences build character and strength.

The Tale of Mia's Magnificent Maze

Mia, a quiet and thoughtful third-grader, sometimes struggled with confidence during group activities. One day, her teacher set up a "maze challenge" on the playground using cones, ropes, and creative markers. Teams had to navigate the maze, and every wrong turn meant starting over. Mia's team encountered several setbacks: wrong turns, disagreements on which path to choose, and moments of frustration. Instead of giving up, Mia took charge by encouraging her teammates to share ideas and reminding them that every mistake was simply part of the learning process. By working together and celebrating small successes, Mia's team eventually completed the maze. Mia's newfound confidence shone through, and her classmates learned that every challenge was an opportunity to grow—even if it meant starting over a few times.

The Soccer Squad's Comeback

In another classroom, a group of fourth-graders formed a mini-soccer league during recess. Initially, games were filled with bickering and frustration whenever things went wrong. One day, after a particularly tough loss, the teacher gathered the team and led a discussion about resilience. The children talked about how each missed goal and defensive error was a chance to learn and improve. Inspired by the conversation, the team decided to change their approach. They began practicing together, encouraging each other, and celebrating every small improvement. Over time, the soccer games transformed into joyful, supportive experiences where every player felt valued. The "Soccer Squad" not only improved their skills but also learned invaluable lessons about teamwork, persistence, and the power of a positive attitude.

The Dance of Determination

In a creative classroom, the teacher introduced a weekly "dance party" where students could express themselves through movement. Initially, some students were hesitant—unsure of how to move or worried about being judged. However, the teacher emphasized that there was no right or wrong way to dance and that the goal was simply to have fun and express oneself. Gradually, the dance party became the highlight of the week. Students experimented with different moves, even creating group routines, and the act of dancing became a powerful outlet for releasing stress and building confidence. Over time, the dance party served as a metaphor for life itself: sometimes you lead, sometimes you follow, but together, you create something beautiful out of movement and expression.

Lessons from the Wild: The Playful World of Lion Cubs

Let's circle back to our earlier inspiration—the playful lion cubs. In the wild, lion cubs spend hours engaged in playful antics that might look chaotic to an observer, but each leap, pounce, and tumble is a carefully orchestrated lesson in survival. These cubs wrestle with each other, practice their pouncing skills, and learn how to navigate their environment. Through play, they develop strength, coordination, and social skills that are critical for their future roles as hunters and leaders. Just as these young animals are building resilience through play, our students are doing the same in their own unique ways.

Every time a lion cub falls during a play fight, it gets back up, learning to push through discomfort and adapt. Similarly, when our students face setbacks—whether it's a block tower that collapses or a game where they don't win—they are developing resilience. These moments teach them how to overcome failure, adapt, and keep going. Just as the cubs refine their hunting skills through play, our students build the inner strength and determination needed to face life's challenges. By supporting them through these playful learning experiences, we're helping them cultivate the resilience they'll need to succeed in both the classroom and life.

Bringing It All Together: Playful Resilience as a Way of Life

The power of play and physical activity goes far beyond just having fun—it is a cornerstone for building resilience. Play isn't just a distraction; it is a dynamic, hands-on way for children to develop the skills they need to overcome life's challenges. Through play, children learn that obstacles can be met with creativity, perseverance, and collaboration. As educators, we have the unique opportunity to create a space where every mistake becomes an opportunity for growth, and every game serves as a lesson in resilience.

The Science Behind the Fun

Let's revisit the science that backs this up. As we discussed in Chapter 2, when children engage in play and physical activity, their brains form new neural connections—this process is called neuroplasticity. This rewiring of the brain makes their minds more flexible and better prepared to navigate future challenges. Every time a child experiments with a new game, faces a group challenge, or even falls down, they are building the mental resilience that will carry them through life's toughest moments. Just like a lion cub's playful pounce builds hunting skills for survival, every playful effort your students make builds the resilience they need to thrive in tomorrow's world.

Building Resilience Through Everyday Moments

Think about the everyday moments in your classroom—whether it's a quick game of "Red Light, Green Light," a cooperative art project, or an outdoor lesson filled with laughter. These moments are not just fun breaks; they are opportunities for resilience to grow. Students learn that setbacks are temporary, that collaboration strengthens us, and that persistence leads to progress. Over time, these everyday experiences build a deep-rooted belief in themselves, that with creativity and perseverance, challenges are meant to be conquered, not avoided.

The Teacher's Role: Championing Playful Resilience

As educators, you are the champions of playful resilience. Your energy, creativity, and ability to embrace play are essential in helping students develop this vital skill. When you join in a game, laugh off a mistake, or celebrate small victories, you show your students that resilience isn't something they're born with—it's something they cultivate every day through play, movement, and a positive mindset. Your role extends beyond teaching academic content; you are shaping resilient spirits that will empower your students to face life's challenges with confidence and strength.

Final Thoughts: Play, Resilience, and the Power of Movement

As we wrap up this chapter, let's take a moment to appreciate the incredible power of play and physical activity in shaping resilient young learners. Whether it's a game of tag, a team challenge, or a playful learning activity, every moment of movement is an opportunity for growth.

We've seen how play helps children develop problem-solving skills, emotional regulation, and teamwork—just like lion cubs honing their survival skills in the wild. We've explored how physical activity builds mental strength, reduces stress, and boosts confidence. And we've discovered simple, actionable ways to bring movement into the classroom, from brain breaks to outdoor learning adventures.

The science behind it all supports this: Play and physical activity play a critical role in developing resilience by strengthening cognitive, emotional, and social abilities. Research by Piaget (1962) and Vygotsky (1978) shows that play is essential for cognitive development, helping children learn problem-solving skills and adapt to challenges. Studies have also shown that physical activity helps to regulate emotions and manage stress, boosting confidence and mental strength. As children engage in play, their brains make important connections that prepare them for future challenges, not just academically, but socially and emotionally.

But beyond the research and strategies, the heart of playful resilience is this: When children are given the freedom to move, explore, and play, they build the inner strength to navigate life's challenges with confidence.

So, as you step into your classroom tomorrow, think about small ways to infuse more movement and play into the day. Whether it's a quick game, a moment of laughter, or a chance for students to lead an activity, these little efforts add up to something powerful—a classroom culture where resilience grows, one playful moment at a time.

So go ahead—let them run, let them jump, let them play. Because in the end, those moments of joy are shaping something far bigger than the game itself. They're shaping stronger, more confident, and more resilient learners—ready to take on the world, one step at a time.

9

Creating a Classroom Culture of Resilience

I've had the privilege of traveling around the world, speaking and working with educators, but one experience stands out—my four-week journey through Malaysia. During my time there, I had the chance to speak with teachers from all over the country and learn from their unique experiences. What struck me most was the deep sense of resilience I witnessed, not just in individuals, but in the way communities came together to support one another.

What makes Malaysia truly unique is its incredible diversity. While the majority of the population is Muslim, the country also has significant Buddhist, Christian, and Hindu communities. The ethnic mosaic, with Malays, Chinese, Indians, and Indigenous groups, contributes to a rich cultural blend. And despite these differences, what amazed me the most was how well people respect and support one another.

I was fortunate to be in Malaysia during the Christmas season, a time of year that, despite the predominantly Muslim population, was celebrated with an openness that reflected the nation's spirit of unity. Christmas decorations were everywhere—in stores, on streets, and even in schools. What touched me deeply was the generosity of the teachers I met, many of whom didn't celebrate

Christmas themselves. Several of them gave me ornaments to hang on my tree when I returned home. It was a beautiful reminder of how, even across cultural and religious differences, kindness and respect flourished. The simple act of sharing these gifts was a powerful reflection of the collective spirit of community that defines resilience in Malaysia.

Back home, as I decorated my tree, each ornament I placed reminded me of the community that embraced me during my travels. These ornaments were more than just holiday decorations; they symbolized the shared experiences and collective spirit of kindness and support that I had witnessed. The act of giving these ornaments wasn't about the religious holiday itself but about the universal language of generosity and community that transcended any barriers.

In Malaysia, resilience wasn't just an individual trait; it was a collective force. I observed how resilience was embedded in everyday practices, from the way meals were shared to the mutual support teachers offered each other. People ate communally, sharing food in ways that fostered connection and solidarity. The act of sharing a meal is a small but powerful example of how resilience thrives in a community that understands the importance of supporting one another. It wasn't just about surviving individually; it was about working together, drawing strength from each other, and lifting one another.

Teachers supported one another not just professionally, but personally, helping each other navigate challenges and difficult situations. In a culture where resilience was built on community rather than isolation, it was clear that when one person faced hardship, the entire community rallied behind them, offering encouragement, help, and solidarity.

This experience reshaped my understanding of resilience. In the classrooms I visited, resilience wasn't just about one student bouncing back from hardship. It was about how the community, whether family, friends, or teachers, came together to support each other through struggles. It wasn't about facing adversity alone—it was about building a network of support that made it possible for everyone to thrive.

In our classrooms, we can take inspiration from this collective strength. Resilience, in its truest form, is not just about facing challenges alone. It's about the strength we gain from the community around us. It's about creating an environment where students don't just survive together; they thrive together. This is the kind of resilience we need to nurture in our students—teaching them that their individual strength is amplified by the support of those around them.

The Power of Peer Recognition

One of the most beautiful aspects of a resilient classroom is that it's a community—a community where everyone's growth is celebrated. This sense of collective progress is key to building resilience because it teaches students that they don't have to face challenges alone. When students recognize and celebrate each other's efforts, they strengthen their belief in their own ability to overcome obstacles.

Imagine a classroom where students high-five each other after a tough test, where they cheer for one another during challenging projects, and where every small victory is recognized. The power of peer recognition cannot be overstated. It's contagious! When students see their peers overcome obstacles, they start to believe that they can do it too. This creates an environment where resilience isn't just something you have to teach—it's something students are actively practicing and reinforcing every day.

Why Peer Recognition Works

Research shows that peer recognition has an incredible impact on students' self-esteem and growth. When students acknowledge each other's progress, it not only boosts the confidence of the one being recognized but also the person doing the recognizing.

In fact, peer recognition fosters a sense of belonging and community, making students feel valued and seen, and this in turn increases their own drive to persist through challenges.

Tips for Building a Resilient Culture

Let's dive into some practical strategies for fostering a culture of resilience in your classroom. These ideas will help you create a space where students are empowered to grow, persevere, and face adversity head-on.

1. Classroom Celebrations: "Resilience Celebrations"
Hold regular "Resilience Celebrations" where students can share stories of challenges they've faced and how they overcame them. This could be as simple as a group discussion, or you could set up a board where students write down their victories and struggles. You might even have a "Resilience Wall," where students can post inspiring quotes or personal stories of perseverance. The key, here, is to make celebrating resilience a regular part of classroom culture so that students get used to acknowledging both their challenges and their growth.

2. Model Resilience Yourself
As a teacher, you have a unique opportunity to model resilience for your students. Share your own stories of struggle and triumph. Let your students see that resilience isn't something you're born with—it's something you can build over time. When you show them that you, too, face challenges and that you keep pushing forward, they'll understand that resilience isn't about avoiding failure—it's about how you handle setbacks and grow from them.

You might say something like, "I know this lesson didn't go as I planned, but here's how I'm going to improve it next time. We all make mistakes, and it's how we respond that matters. I'm going to keep learning, and so can you."

3. Encourage Collaboration

Group activities where students work together to solve problems or overcome obstacles can help build both their resilience and their social-emotional skills. When students work together to tackle a challenge, they learn how to navigate setbacks as a team, reinforcing the idea that perseverance isn't just an individual trait—it's something you can lean on others for.

Whether it's group problem-solving tasks or team-building exercises, collaboration helps students practice communication, patience, and persistence—skills that will serve them in every area of life.

Practical Ways to Foster a Resilient Culture in Your Classroom

So, how can you really make resilience a core part of your classroom? Here are some concrete ideas for creating an environment where students are empowered to push through adversity.

1. Weekly Reflection Circles

Every week, set aside time for students to reflect on their own challenges and growth. You could have them write in journals or participate in group discussions. Ask them to share one challenge they overcame during the week, and how they managed to do so. This reflection time doesn't just encourage resilience—it helps students develop self-awareness, as they reflect on how they handled difficulties and what they learned from them.

In addition, you might want to prompt them with questions like, "What did you do when you felt stuck? Who helped you along the way?" This kind of reflection helps students understand that challenges are a natural part of life and that there's always something to be learned from every obstacle they face.

2. Resilience Awards

It's important to celebrate resilience, but that doesn't mean rewarding perfection. Instead, focus on persistence and effort.

Consider creating a "Resilience Star" award for the student who has demonstrated the most growth in a given week, regardless of whether they succeeded in every task or goal. This can be an opportunity to recognize not just academic achievement, but personal progress. Maybe a student struggled with a math problem all week but finally solved it—or perhaps another student faced a personal challenge but continued to show up and do their best. These stories of resilience deserve recognition.

3. Interactive Challenges

A great way to build resilience is by incorporating small, fun challenges that require students to think critically and persist through frustration. Puzzle challenges, group brainstorming sessions, and team-building games all offer opportunities for students to practice problem-solving, teamwork, and perseverance. These activities show students that failure is not the end—it's simply part of the process of learning and growing.

Incorporating Cultural Representation and Diversity in Building Resilience

When we talk about resilience, we need to remember that it doesn't look the same for every child. Resilience is deeply influenced by a student's cultural background, personal experiences, and environment. As educators, we have the responsibility to ensure that our approach to resilience reflects the diverse identities and lived experiences of our students. Different cultures can have distinct ways of handling challenges, and the way students respond to adversity may reflect their cultural norms and values. For example, in some cultures, staying quiet or appearing stoic during difficulties may be a sign of strength, even if others perceive it as struggling.

By incorporating cultural relevance into your teaching, you're not just making your classroom more inclusive—you're empowering your students to see themselves as capable and resilient. When students see their own stories reflected in the curriculum, they're more likely to believe in their own potential to succeed.

Why Representation Matters

Representation is more than just a buzzword—it's a powerful tool for fostering resilience. When students can see people who look like them, share their experiences, and understand their challenges, they start to believe that overcoming obstacles is possible for them, too. Whether it's race, ethnicity, socioeconomic background, gender, or family structure, students need to see themselves reflected in the stories, materials, and lessons they engage with.

For example, a young girl growing up in a single-parent household might find strength in reading about other children facing similar struggles, or a student from an immigrant background might feel empowered after learning about characters who overcame challenges related to adjusting to a new culture or language.

Practical Ways to Integrate Diverse Representation

Here are some strategies for ensuring that your classroom reflects the diverse cultural backgrounds of your students and incorporates resilience into the curriculum in a meaningful way.

1. Diverse Literature

Stock your classroom library with books that feature diverse characters, cultures, and experiences. Include books that reflect a wide range of cultural backgrounds, family dynamics, socioeconomic statuses, gender roles, and even neurodiversity. The goal is to choose books that show resilience as a core theme—whether it's overcoming personal adversity, persevering through systemic challenges, or navigating identity struggles.

Books like *The Name Jar* by Yangsook Choi (about a young immigrant girl adjusting to a new school) and *I Am Enough* by Grace Byers (a celebration of self-love and resilience) can be powerful tools for fostering a resilient mindset. Provide stories that resonate with your students, helping them see that resilience is something they can build, too.

2. Celebrate Cultural Holidays and Traditions

Take time throughout the year to celebrate a variety of cultural holidays, customs, and traditions. Recognizing these events helps students feel that their cultural heritage is valued and respected in the classroom. Celebrating Black History Month, Hispanic Heritage Month, and Asian Pacific American Heritage Month are great opportunities to highlight the resilience of different communities.

Additionally, you can learn about religious holidays such as Diwali, Hanukkah, Ramadan, and Christmas. This not only helps students learn about each other's traditions but also fosters a sense of empathy and understanding, which are key components of resilience.

3. Invite Guest Speakers

Bring in guest speakers from different cultural backgrounds to share their stories of resilience. These guests could be community leaders, local historians, or even parents willing to talk about their cultural heritage. Guest speakers provide students with real-world examples of resilience, making the concept come alive and demonstrating its practical application.

4. Use Music and Art

Music and art are universal languages that can help students connect with different cultures and explore themes of resilience. Introduce songs from various cultural traditions that reflect perseverance, hope, and overcoming adversity. You might explore traditional African drumming, Latin American folk music, or

Asian melodies that speak to the struggles and triumphs of the people who created them.

Art projects inspired by cultural artists can also be a fun way to explore resilience. Through art, students can learn about different cultural perspectives on perseverance, gaining a deeper appreciation for the resilience of people around the world.

Embracing Cultural Contexts in Resilience Building

When sharing resilience stories, it's essential to recognize that the challenges children face are often deeply rooted in their cultural context. A child's resilience is shaped by their community, history, and familial values. For this reason, stories of resilience should reflect the diverse cultures of your students. Recognizing cultural differences helps validate each student's journey and shows them that resilience is an inclusive trait that transcends boundaries.

Resilience doesn't look the same for every child. It is deeply influenced by a student's cultural background, personal experiences, and environment. As educators, we have the responsibility to ensure that our approach to resilience reflects the diverse identities and lived experiences of our students.

In collectivist cultures, such as those often found in East Asia, Latin America, and some parts of Africa, resilience is often seen in terms of the group rather than the individual. Students in these cultures may be more likely to rely on family and community support during difficult times, and resilience may be understood as persevering for the well-being of the collective group (Chiu & Hong, 2006). These students may feel a stronger motivation to continue overcoming challenges, knowing that their success contributes to the strength and honor of their community.

Conversely, individualistic cultures, such as those commonly found in Western countries, may emphasize personal autonomy and individual perseverance. In these cultures, students may view resilience as a personal trait to be cultivated and tested against individual challenges (Markus & Kitayama, 1991). These students may be more likely to feel the pressure to succeed for themselves, but the emphasis on individual achievement can sometimes make it harder for them to ask for help or rely on the collective.

As educators, it's crucial to be mindful of these cultural differences in how resilience is understood. By recognizing that students from different backgrounds may approach challenges in unique ways, we can offer them the support they need in culturally relevant ways. Integrating culturally responsive teaching practices that honor both collectivist and individualistic viewpoints can help build a more inclusive classroom where all students feel empowered to be resilient in ways that align with their cultural values (Gay, 2010).

3 Tips for Building a Resilient Classroom Culture with a Focus on Diversity

Building a classroom environment that embraces diversity and promotes resilience requires intentional effort. Here are three practical strategies for integrating cultural relevance and enhancing resilience in your classroom:

1. **Celebrate Diverse Stories of Resilience**
   Integrate books, resources, and lessons that reflect the diverse cultural backgrounds of your students. By showcasing resilience through the lens of different cultures and experiences, students can see themselves in the stories, which strengthens their belief in their own ability to persevere. Stories from various cultural contexts—such as overcoming personal adversity, battling systemic injustice, or navigating identity struggles—help students realize that resilience comes in many forms.
2. **Foster an Inclusive Community**
   Create a classroom environment where every student's unique cultural background is valued. Encourage students to share their personal experiences of overcoming obstacles, whether from their home life, culture,

or community. This not only strengthens resilience but also promotes empathy and understanding among peers. When students learn to appreciate each other's challenges and triumphs, they build a strong, supportive network that encourages perseverance.

3. **Model Cultural Sensitivity in Resilience**
   As a teacher, model how resilience is shaped by cultural contexts. Recognize that different students may face unique challenges due to their backgrounds and show how these challenges can be opportunities for growth. Support students in understanding that resilience is not one-size-fits-all—it's rooted in the experiences and values of each individual. By acknowledging the role of culture in shaping a student's resilience, you help them feel understood and empowered to face adversity in their own way.

Final Thoughts: Embracing Collective Strength and Cultural Resilience

As we wrap up our exploration of creating a culture of resilience, it is essential to remember that resilience, at its core, is not merely about overcoming individual obstacles—it's about drawing strength from the collective. The story of Malaysia's resilient communities reminds us that resilience is woven into the fabric of connection and mutual support. It's about building a network of support—whether it's through peer recognition, shared meals, or the deep cultural respect that fosters unity across differences.

As educators, our role is to create an environment where students know they are not alone in their struggles. By embracing the power of community, we can help them build resilience not just as a skill, but as a mindset—a way of being that is shaped by the collective strength of those around them. Whether through recognizing each other's efforts, celebrating cultural diversity, or modeling perseverance, we are empowering our students to face challenges head-on with the knowledge that they have a network that believes in them and supports them.

In the end, resilience is a practice that must be nurtured every day. It requires intentional actions, both big and small, to create an environment where students feel seen, heard, and valued. It thrives in spaces where failure is not feared but embraced as part of the journey toward growth. And, most importantly, it flourishes in communities that celebrate each other's victories, big and small. So, let's continue to build classrooms where resilience is not just taught—it's lived, celebrated, and shared, one step at a time.

10
Resilience: A Blueprint for Adapting to a Changing World

In *Back to the Future Part II*, Marty McFly travels to the future, a world filled with flying cars, hoverboards, and advanced technology. At first, Marty is excited about the changes but quickly realizes that the future is much more unpredictable and confusing than he anticipated. The world he encounters is different from the one he knew in 1985, and he has to adapt to everything from futuristic gadgets to new social dynamics.

One key moment comes when Marty tries to use a hoverboard to escape from a gang of bullies. He quickly learns that although the hoverboard is a cool piece of technology, it's also more difficult to control than anything he's used before. The first time he tries it, he falls flat on his face. But instead of giving up, Marty perseveres, learns from his mistakes, and improves his technique. He adapts to the new technology and uses it to navigate through the challenges he faces.

Marty's resilience is tested again when he has to confront Biff Tannen, who has used the sports almanac to manipulate events and change the future. Marty must adapt quickly to this new reality, where things aren't as predictable as they used to be. By adjusting his approach, learning from his past mistakes, and keeping an open mind, Marty manages to set things right and restore the timeline.

This experience shows how adaptability and resilience are essential when facing the unknown. Just like Marty McFly, students today need to develop the ability to adjust to rapidly changing environments, learn from failures, and persevere through challenges. The world that Marty encountered in the movie is not so different from the world today: one full of new technologies, shifting career paths, and changing societal expectations. The lessons of adaptability and resilience that Marty learned are the same ones that will prepare students to thrive in a future that is unpredictable and constantly evolving.

As we prepare students for this ever-changing world, educators must focus not just on academic skills, but on nurturing the adaptability and resilience necessary to face unforeseen challenges. Like Marty, students need to learn how to adjust quickly, embrace new tools and situations, and persevere even when things don't go as planned. This kind of resilience—adaptable resilience—will be the key to success in a future that is bound to be as full of unexpected twists and turns as Marty's adventure in the future. By fostering this mindset in our classrooms, we help students become better equipped to navigate the uncertainties of the world ahead.

The Evolution of Resilience: Adapting to the New Reality

In the past, resilience meant enduring the challenges of a long, stable career. Many people graduated from school, found a job, worked in it for 30 to 40 years, and retired. The world they navigated was relatively predictable: Jobs had fixed titles, industries remained stable, and the roadmap from education to career was straightforward. However, the world today looks vastly different. Industries are evolving at unprecedented speeds, technology is transforming the landscape of nearly every profession, and careers are far less linear. The future is uncertain, and the traditional idea of resilience, which focuses on persistence through long-term stability, is no longer sufficient.

In today's world, resilience has become more than just the ability to endure—resilience now demands adaptability. It's not about clinging to outdated paradigms of success but learning to thrive in an ever-changing environment. Today's students must be equipped with the skills, mindset, and tools to be resilient in ways that were not necessary for previous generations. They must be prepared to navigate change, face the unknown, and develop the ability to pivot and learn continuously. Resilience, in the context of the modern world, means embracing change, leveraging new opportunities, and being able to adapt to unforeseen circumstances.

Resilience Defined: From Endurance to Adaptability

Traditionally, resilience was often seen as the ability to persist through adversity. People who were resilient could endure tough times, push through difficulty, and keep going despite challenges. For decades, this definition of resilience was sufficient because the world around us moved at a slower pace. Careers were defined by stability, and if you worked hard and did your job well, you could expect to stay in the same position for decades.

Today, however, the very concept of a career is changing. Many industries that once promised lifelong employment are now in flux, disrupted by technology and globalization. The average person today can expect to change jobs multiple times, and the very idea of a "job for life" is becoming increasingly rare (Brynjolfsson & McAfee, 2014). The skills needed for future success are no longer based on memorizing facts and performing repetitive tasks; they are centered around creativity, problem-solving, emotional intelligence, and adaptability. Students need resilience to thrive in an environment where flexibility, creativity, and innovation are the currencies of success.

The traditional idea of resilience—grit, perseverance, and staying the course—still holds value, but it must now be expanded to include the ability to pivot, learn new skills quickly, and embrace uncertainty. The resilience of the future will look different. It will not be about simply enduring difficult circumstances but about continuously adapting to them, leveraging new opportunities, and making the most of the changing world around us.

The Changing Nature of Work: Embracing Uncertainty and Adaptability

One of the biggest shifts in today's world is how work itself has changed. The rise of artificial intelligence (AI), automation, and globalization has created a new landscape for the workforce. Jobs that once seemed secure are now being replaced by machines or automated processes, and new jobs are emerging that didn't even exist a decade ago (Frey & Osborne, 2017). As industries evolve, so must the workers who drive them. No longer is it enough for students to prepare for one type of career; they need to be ready for careers that may not yet exist or that may require them to continuously upskill as technology changes.

This is where resilience takes on new meaning. In the past, resilience was often associated with enduring a fixed job. Now, it must be about preparing students to face uncertainty, uncertainty that comes from rapidly changing industries, fluctuating job markets, and new technological innovations. Students must learn how to develop the skills to not only survive in a dynamic environment but to thrive in it. They must be taught how to adapt, be resourceful, and stay flexible in the face of a constantly shifting job market.

The ability to adapt is now one of the most crucial skills in the 21st century. As new technologies are implemented and entire industries are transformed, adaptable students will be best positioned to succeed. Educators must teach students to embrace a mindset of flexibility, showing them that resilience is not about stubbornly clinging to a path but about finding new paths when the old ones no longer work. Resilient students must be prepared for a world where jobs are not guaranteed, careers may change, and the future is full of possibilities that require new thinking and new skills.

Preparing for an Unpredictable Future: The Role of Education in Building Resilience

Given the rapidly changing world we live in, the role of education must also evolve. Schools have traditionally focused on preparing students for stable careers by teaching foundational knowledge and skills. However, to thrive in today's world, students need more than just academic knowledge; they need the ability to learn continuously, adapt to new situations, and solve problems creatively.

This shift requires that schools emphasize not just what students learn, but how they learn. It's no longer enough to focus on rote memorization or standardized test scores. In the modern world, students must be equipped to think critically, collaborate with others, and develop the skills needed to adapt to ever-changing circumstances. Schools must teach students how to learn, not just what to learn. This includes fostering a growth mindset, encouraging students to see challenges as opportunities to grow, and teaching them how to use failure as a learning experience rather than a setback.

The power of adaptability is clear in the context of today's rapidly changing world. For example, in industries such as technology, healthcare, and business, employees are expected to keep learning new skills as tools and techniques evolve. A resilient student is one who not only embraces challenges but also seeks them out, knowing that each new experience is an opportunity to grow and develop. This mindset can be cultivated through education by encouraging students to experiment, fail, and learn from those failures in a safe and supportive environment.

Developing Adaptable Resilience

In today's world, the ability to adapt to constant change is more critical than ever. To equip students for the future, we must create opportunities for them to develop adaptable resilience. This resilience helps them navigate challenges both inside and outside the classroom, preparing them for an ever-evolving landscape of education, careers, and life itself.

Here are activities that can help elementary students build this crucial skill:

1. Growth Mindset Challenges
- **Activity**: Encourage students to tackle challenging tasks that push them out of their comfort zones, such as solving difficult puzzles or writing creatively. When students face these tasks, remind them that struggling is part of learning, and success often comes through persistence.
- **How to Apply**: After completing the task, have students reflect on the strategies that helped them push through. Emphasizing the value of perseverance and adapting strategies fosters resilience and prepares them for future challenges where the path to success isn't always clear-cut.

2. Resilience Journals
- **Activity**: Have students keep a "resilience journal" where they document obstacles they've faced—whether in school, social situations, or at home—and how they adapted or overcame them. They can reflect on moments of frustration and the strategies they used to regain composure and continue.
- **How to Apply**: The journal becomes a tool for self-reflection, allowing students to track their growth and adapt strategies for future challenges. It fosters emotional resilience and adaptability by helping students understand their emotional responses and learn from them.

3. Group Problem-Solving Activities
- **Activity**: Assign collaborative tasks where students must work together to solve problems or complete projects. For example, designing a solution to a fictional challenge or creating a team presentation. These activities require flexibility and adaptability in managing different opinions and approaches.

- **How to Apply**: Students will learn to compromise, adjust their approaches, and collaborate effectively, which helps build resilience in social and academic contexts. Encouraging reflection after these activities allows students to see how they can adapt their approach to be more effective in the future.

4. Role-Playing Scenarios
- **Activity**: Use role-playing to simulate real-life challenges such as losing a game, dealing with disappointment, or facing a setback in schoolwork. Guide students through these scenarios, discussing how to adapt and persevere.
- **How to Apply**: This teaches emotional resilience and adaptability by helping students practice their responses in low-stakes scenarios before facing real-world setbacks. It encourages flexibility in problem-solving and dealing with disappointment.

5. Resilience Through Physical Challenges
- **Activity**: Incorporate physical challenges like obstacle courses, balance exercises, or cooperative games where students need to rely on each other and push themselves beyond their comfort zones.
- **How to Apply**: As students face physical obstacles, they practice perseverance and adaptability in a hands-on way. Teachers should reinforce the idea that pushing through difficulty builds strength and resilience, both physically and mentally.

6. "No-Excuse" Projects
- **Activity**: Assign long-term projects with strict deadlines but introduce a "no-excuse" policy. If a student is absent, for example, they must find ways to stay on track. This teaches that life's obstacles—like illness or unexpected challenges—are not excuses for failure.
- **How to Apply**: Students learn to adapt to changes in their schedule, handle obstacles, and persevere through difficulties, developing resilience to navigate the unpredictability of life and work.

7. The Resilience Quest: Adventure Learning
- **Activity**: Create an "adventure" within the classroom where students must work together to solve clues, complete tasks, or unlock a final mystery. Each stage of the adventure represents an obstacle they need to overcome, whether physical, creative, or intellectual.
- **How to Apply**: As they face these challenges, students apply problem-solving, creative thinking, and teamwork. This teaches adaptability because students will need to adjust their strategies based on the nature of each obstacle.

8. Building the Resilience Bridge
- **Activity**: Have students design and build a bridge using materials like popsicle sticks, glue, or paper. The challenge is to design a structure that can hold a specific weight, but when it fails, students must analyze what went wrong and make adjustments.
- **How to Apply**: This hands-on activity teaches students that failure is part of learning. Through iterative design, students learn how to adapt and improve their approach, a critical skill for resilience in both academic and real-world scenarios.

9. "What If?" Scenarios
- **Activity**: Present students with a series of "What if?" scenarios, such as "What if the class project is due tomorrow, and you're not finished?" or "What if you and your group are having trouble agreeing?" Ask students to brainstorm solutions for these hypothetical situations.
- **How to Apply**: This exercise encourages students to think critically about how they might react to setbacks and challenges, reinforcing adaptability. It also helps them realize that they have the power to shape their responses and overcome obstacles.

Integrating Adaptable Resilience into Everyday Learning

By integrating these activities into their daily classroom routine, teachers can help students develop adaptable resilience. These exercises don't just prepare students to face challenges within the school environment but also equip them with the mental flexibility needed to thrive in an ever-changing world. Developing adaptability is not just about helping students bounce back after failure but encouraging them to learn how to adjust and succeed despite the unpredictability that life and work often present.

By framing resilience as a set of adaptable skills that can be learned and strengthened over time, teachers can empower students with the confidence to face any challenge, now and in the future.

The Role of Educators: Modeling Resilience and Adaptability

Teachers themselves must also model resilience and adaptability. As educators, we must embrace the same qualities we hope to instill in our students. This means being open to new teaching methods, continuously learning, and adjusting to meet the needs of students in a changing environment. When students see teachers adapting to new challenges and remaining calm and composed in the face of adversity, they learn to mirror these behaviors in their own lives.

Teachers must be transparent about their own struggles and how they overcome them. By sharing stories of how they navigate challenges—whether it's adjusting to new curriculum standards, implementing new technology, or overcoming personal difficulties—educators can show students that resilience is not about being perfect but about persevering and growing. When students see their teachers persist through difficulties, it reinforces the idea that challenges are an inevitable part of life, but they are also opportunities for growth.

 ### Final Thoughts: The Future of Resilience in Education

In the past, resilience was defined as the ability to endure long periods of stability and overcome hardships within a predictable framework. Today, however, resilience requires much more: It demands adaptability, flexibility, and a continuous commitment to learning and evolving. The future is uncertain, but students who develop resilience—the ability to face challenges, pivot when needed, and thrive in the face of adversity—will be best positioned for success.

As educators, we must prepare our students for a future that is as unpredictable as it is exciting. We must teach them not only the academic knowledge they need but also the skills that will allow them to thrive in an ever-changing world. This means cultivating a culture of adaptability, critical thinking, creativity, and emotional intelligence. By doing so, we will equip students with the tools they need to not only survive but to flourish in a world full of possibility.

A memorable line from *Back to the Future* has always stuck with me: "Roads? Where we're going, we don't need roads." When Doc Brown says this, he's acknowledging that the future is not only unknown, but it's also evolving so quickly that the rules of the past no longer apply. That simple line, so iconic, speaks volumes about how swiftly things can change, how we need to be ready for the unknown, and how much adaptability will be required. The future, like Marty and Doc's time-traveling adventures, is full of twists and turns we can't yet predict.

The future belongs to those who can bend, shift, and adapt—not to those who cling to the past. We are not just preparing students to face the world; we are preparing them to transform it. The resilience we foster today will shape the leaders, innovators, and visionaries of tomorrow. So, as we move forward, let us ensure that the resilience we build in our classrooms is not just about enduring—it's about thriving in a future we can't yet fully imagine, but one that our students will help create.

Let's build that future together, one resilient, adaptable student at a time.

References

Anderson, C. (2020). *Oprah: A biography*. Penguin Press.

Angelou, M. (2008). *Letter to my daughter*. Random House.

Berk, L. E. (2013). *Child development* (9th ed.). Pearson Education.

Blackwell, L. S., Trzesniewski, K. H., & Dweck, C. S. (2007). Implicit theories of intelligence predict achievement across an adolescent transition: A longitudinal study and an intervention. *Child Development*, 78(1), 246–263.

Bodrova, E., & Leong, D. J. (2007). The importance of play in promoting healthy child development and maintaining strong parent-child bonds. *American Journal of Play*, 3(1), 61–82.

Boyatzis, R. E., Goleman, D., & Rhee, K. (2000). Clustering competence in emotional intelligence: Insights from the Emotional Competence Inventory (ECI). In R. Bar-On & J. D. A. Parker (Eds.), *Handbook of emotional intelligence* (pp. 343–362). Jossey-Bass.

Bradberry, T., & Greaves, J. (2009). *Emotional intelligence 2.0*. TalentSmart.

Brynjolfsson, E., & McAfee, A. (2014). *The second machine age: Work, progress, and prosperity in a time of brilliant technologies*. W.W. Norton & Company.

Burdette, H. L., & Whitaker, R. C. (2005). Resurrecting free play in young children: Looking beyond fitness and fatness to attention, affiliation, and affect. *Journal of Pediatrics, 116*(6), 1567–1574.

Byers, G. (2018). *I am enough*. HarperOne.

Cherniss, C., & Goleman, D. (2001). *The emotionally intelligent workplace: How to select for, measure, and improve emotional intelligence in individuals, groups, and organizations*. Jossey-Bass.

Choi, Y. (2001). *The Name Jar*. Dragonfly Books.

Dweck, C. S. (2006). *Mindset: The new psychology of success*. Random House.

Ewing, M. E., Goc Karp, G., & Brown, D. L. (2002). *Teaching social responsibility through physical activity*. Human Kinetics.

Frey, C. B., & Osborne, M. A. (2017). The future of employment: How susceptible are jobs to computerization? *Technological Forecasting* and *Social Change,* 114, 254–280. https://doi.org/10.1016/j.techfore.2016.08.019

Friedman, M. (2018). *Relational intelligence: The new essential skill for leaders.* Wiley.

Gay, G. (2010). *Culturally responsive teaching: Theory, research, and practice* (2nd ed.). Teachers College Press.

Ginsburg, K. R. (2007). The importance of play in promoting healthy child development and maintaining strong parent-child bonds. *Pediatrics*, 119(1), 182–191.

Ginsburg, K. R., & Committee on Communications and Committee on Psychosocial Aspects of Child and Family Health. (2007). The importance of play in promoting healthy child development and maintaining strong parent-child bonds. *Pediatrics*, 119(1), 182–191.

Goleman, D. (1995). *Emotional intelligence: Why it can matter more than IQ.* Bantam Books.

Gray, P. (2013). *Free to learn: Why unleashing the instinct to play will make our children happier, more self-reliant, and better students for life.* Basic Books.

Greenberg, M. T., Domitrovich, C. E., & Bumbarger, B. (2003). The prevention of mental disorders in school-aged children: A review of the effectiveness of prevention programs. *Prevention & Treatment*, 6(1), 1–91.

Hillman, C. H., Erickson, K. I., & Kramer, A. F. (2008). Be smart, exercise your heart: Exercise effects on brain and cognition. *Nature Reviews Neuroscience*, 9(1), 58–65.

Huebner, E. S., Suldo, S. M., & Valois, R. F. (2004). The role of self-report in the development of emotional regulation in children and adolescents. *Journal of School Psychology,* 42(5), 299–313.

Kelley, S. (2015). The rise of Oprah Winfrey: Emotional intelligence as leadership. *Harvard Business Review*, 93(4), 52–59.

Markus, H. R., & Kitayama, S. (1991). Culture and the self: Implications for cognition, emotion, and motivation. *Psychological Review,* 98(2), 224–253.

Michl, L. C., McLaughlin, K. A., Shepherd, K., & Nolen-Hoeksema, S. (2013). Rumination as a mechanism linking stressful life events to symptoms of depression and anxiety: Longitudinal evidence in early adolescents and adults. *Journal of Abnormal Psychology*, 122(2), 339–335.

Murray, N., & Ramstetter, C. (2013). The crucial role of recess in school. *Pediatrics*, 131(1), 183–188.

Northouse, P. G. (2018). *Leadership: Theory and practice* (8th ed.). Sage Publications.

Pellis, S. M., & Pellis, V. C. (2009). *The playful brain: Venturing to the limits of neuroscience.* Oxford University Press.

Perry, B. D., & Szalavitz, M. (2006). *The boy who was raised as a dog: And other stories from a child psychiatrist's notebook.* Basic Books.

Piaget, J. (1962). *Play, dreams, and imitation in childhood.* Norton.

Salmon, P. (2001). Effects of physical activity on depression and anxiety. *The Canadian Journal of Psychiatry*, 46(10), 506–514.

Sari, H., & Tabak, I. (2017). The role of self-regulation and physical activity in school-aged children's emotional well-being. *Journal of School Health,* 87(9), 676–683.

Seligman, M. E. P. (2011). *Flourish: A visionary new understanding of happiness and well-being.* Free Press.

Seligman, M. E. P. (2011). *Learned optimism: How to change your mind and your life.* Vintage.

Sharma, M. (2019). *Resilience: The science of mastering life's greatest challenges.* Springer.

Singh, N. A., Clements, K., & Fiatarone, M. A. (2008). The efficacy of exercise as a long-term antidepressant in elderly subjects: A randomized controlled trial. *The Journals of Gerontology Series A: Biological Sciences and Medical Sciences*, 53(3), 158–165.

Snyder, M., & Omoto, A. M. (2015). Understanding the role of group membership in resilience. *Psychological Science*, 26(7), 980–987.

Sze, J. A., & Herring, M. P. (2017). Effects of mindfulness and breathing techniques on stress reduction in children. *Psychological Science,* 28(6), 798–805.

Vygotsky, L. S. (1978). *Mind in society: The development of higher psychological processes* (M. Cole, V. John-Steiner, S. Scribner, & E. Souberman, Eds.). Harvard University Press.

Yeager, D. S., & Dweck, C. S. (2012). Mindsets that promote resilience: When students believe that personal characteristics can be developed. *Educational Psychologist*, 47(4), 302–314. doi:10.1080/00461520.2012.732020

Zaccaro, A., O'Driscoll, D. M., & Salas, E. (2018). The effects of breathing techniques on the physiological and psychological responses to stress. *Journal of Applied Psychology,* 103(6), 602–616.

Zeidan, F., Johnson, S. K., Diamond, B. J., & David, Z. (2010). Mindfulness meditation improves cognition: Evidence of brief mental training. *Consciousness and Cognition,* 19(2), 1045–1052.

Zemeckis, R. (Director). (1989). *Back to the Future Part II* [Film]. Universal Pictures.

For Product Safety Concerns and Information please contact our EU
representative GPSR@taylorandfrancis.com
Taylor & Francis Verlag GmbH, Kaufingerstraße 24, 80331 München, Germany

www.ingramcontent.com/pod-product-compliance
Lightning Source LLC
Chambersburg PA
CBHW070740230426
43669CB00014B/2523